ULI on the Future
Creating More Livable Metropolitan Areas

Underwritten in part by:

Walt Disney Imagineering

E&Y Kenneth Leventhal
Real Estate Group
ERNST & YOUNG LLP

MORGAN STANLEY DEAN WITTER

Prudential Home Building Investors, Inc.

P H B I

ULI

Urban Land
Institute

About ULI–the Urban Land Institute

ULI–the Urban Land Institute is a nonprofit education and research institute that is supported and directed by its members. Its mission is to provide responsible leadership in the use of land in order to enhance the total environment.

ULI sponsors educational programs and forums to encourage an open international exchange of ideas and sharing of experience; initiates research that anticipates emerging land use trends and issues and proposes creative solutions based on this research; provides advisory services; and publishes a wide variety of materials to disseminate information on land use and development.

Established in 1936, the Institute today has some 13,000 members and associates from more than 50 countries representing the entire spectrum of the land use and development disciplines. They include developers, builders, property owners, investors, architects, public officials, planners, real estate brokers, appraisers, attorneys, engineers, financiers, academics, students, and librarians. ULI members contribute to higher standards of land use by sharing their knowledge and experience. The Institute has long been recognized as one of America's most respected and widely quoted sources of objective information on urban planning, growth, and development.

Richard M. Rosan
Executive Vice President

Recommended bibliographic listing:
ULI–the Urban Land Institute. *ULI on the Future: Creating More Livable Metropolitan Areas.* Washington, D.C.: ULI–the Urban Land Institute, 1997.

ULI Catalog Number: U09
International Standard Book Number: 087420-810-6
List Price: $24.95 ULI Members • $49.95 Nonmembers

ULI Officers

Report Research Staff

Rachelle L. Levitt
Senior Vice President, Research, Education, and Publications

Dean Schwanke
Project Director, ULI on the Future

Gayle L. Berens
Director, University Education, Real Estate School, and Innner-City Research

J. Thomas Black
Resident Fellow, ULI

Lloyd Bookout
Director, Housing and Community Development Research

Jo Allen Gause
Director, Office/Industrial Development Research

Report Production Staff

Frank H. Spink, Jr.
Vice President, Publisher

Nancy H. Stewart
Managing Editor

Carol E. Soble
Copy Editor

Helene Y. Redmond, HYR Graphics
Layout/Design

Betsy Van Buskirk
Cover Design

Diann Stanley-Austin
Production Manager

Ronnie Van Alstyne
Joanne Nanez
Word Processors

Contents

Foreword

As the 20th century closes, competition for residents and employers is increasing among metropolitan regions. Creative development solutions are helping public and private leaders attract and keep people in their communities.

This year's *ULI on the Future*, entitled *Creating More Livable Metropolitan Areas*, features innovative solutions such as infill housing, urban open spaces, the reuse of obsolete buildings, and creating "community" in the suburbs. These particular initiatives also are placed in the broader context of current metropolitan growth patterns and their implications.

Creating More Livable Metropolitan Areas is the fifth edition of ULI's report on the economic and social forces shaping land use. The trends examined in this volume affect all practitioners in real estate development and show that, despite the persistent challenges of modern urban life, opportunities exist and real progress can be made.

The 1997 *ULI on the Future* extends the tradition built by this annual series for distilling the leading thinking on these overarching issues. Our companies are honored to help bring you this edition.

Kenneth P. Wong
President
Walt Disney Imagineering

William M. Lewis, Jr.
Managing Director
Morgan Stanley

Stan Ross
Vice Chair and Managing Partner
E&Y Kenneth Leventhal Real Estate Group

Robert R. Kilroy
Managing Director
Prudential Home Building Investors, Inc.

Creating More Livable Metropolitan Areas

Introduction

Major metropolitan areas around the country must address numerous challenges today if they expect to remain viable and attractive places for their citizens in the future. As most major metropolitan areas continue to grow, they are increasingly viewed as less-than-ideal places to live. Crime, sprawl, traffic congestion, high housing costs, deteriorating central cities, lack of community and sense of place, disappearing open space, and too few attractive parks are just a few of the complaints frequently registered. Too often, the most important asset of large metropolitan areas is the variety and quality of the employment opportunties they offer; many households would choose to live in smaller communities if they could find appropriate employment. This year's *ULI on the Future* focuses on the problems facing metropolitan areas—especially large areas—and what can be done to make our metropolises more livable and less alienating.

In the first article, Lloyd W. Bookout addresses the issue of *community* in suburban areas and highlights numerous ideas and trends that are being used to foster community in new suburban developments. In recent years, he notes, America's suburbs have come under criticism for being socially sterile, socioeconomically exclusive, and lacking a sense of place and identity. Leading this charge and capturing much national media attention have been the proponents of the neo-traditional planning movement—or the so-called *new urbanists*. This article examines the criticisms directed at how new communities have been—and are being—developed. It also explores how forward-thinking developers are changing their development practices in pursuit of a greater sense of *community* and *place*. The article explores recent trends in community development, design, and social programming.

In the second article, Diane R. Suchman tackles the issue of infill housing, especialy in central-city areas, and what can be done to improve inner-city neighborhoods. America's metropolitan areas, she emphasizes, have undergone dramatic economic, demographic, and land use changes over the past 30 years. The article explores the effect of those changes on central cities, the need for public and private action to reinvigorate urban cores, and within this context, the development of infill housing in city neighborhoods.

In the third article, Jo Allen Gause assesses the fate of functionally obsolete commercial buildings that increasingly populate our central cities and that will, in part, determine whether those cities can once again become thriving urban communities. The hoped-for solution is to find feasible alternative uses for structurally sound but otherwise obsolete buildings; bringing dying buildings back to life also brings life back to the city. Though the challenges and risks are formidable, more building owners and developers than ever before are finding opportunities to convert obsolete buildings to desirable and profitable new uses. The most encouraging reasons to believe there will be more feasible building reuse opportunities in the future, Gause notes, are a growing market niche for urban living and working, the increasing use of business improvement districts, and incentives from local governments to help reduce redevelopment costs.

Alexander Garvin addresses the issue of parks and open space in the fourth article. Developing and managing our urban parks and open space have long involved conflicting objectives. While citizens proclaim their love of parks, park budgets are the first to be cut during a fiscal squeeze, leaving many parks in a state of benign neglect. The public's ambivalence is driven in part by its lack of understanding about how to value these assets as long-term qualitative amenities. The article traces the history of park development in the United States, highlights the obstacles to effective park development that have arisen in recent decades, and outlines some solutions for the future, including a renewed emphasis on public funding of park development.

In the fifth and final article, J. Thomas Black looks at the pros and cons of current metropolitan growth patterns. The continued decentralization of metropolitan development in the form of the extended low-density residential areas built around low-density, suburban commercial enclaves has generated many questions about the appropriateness of prevailing development patterns. Since much of the recent literature has tended to emphasize the negative aspects of current patterns, this article makes an effort to look at both the advantages and disadvantages with reference to efforts to measure them where possible.

These articles address only a few of the many issues involved in metropolitan growth and development; the subject is broad and complex, opinions regarding the nature and severity of the problems vary, and solutions are difficult because they must be technically effective, socially productive, economically feasible, and politically acceptable—a tall order. In short, the problems and solutions are about creating a better society, an age-old endeavor that has yielded many improvements in the quality of life in many countries over the last millennium—but no perfect model yet.

Dean Schwanke
Project Director and Editor, *ULI on the Future*

Building Community in America's Suburbs

Lloyd W. Bookout

Lloyd W. Bookout is director of housing and community development research at ULI and the author of ULI's *Residential Development Handbook.* He is currently directing research on master-planned communities and multifamily housing.

In recent years, America's suburbs have become the target of considerable criticism. "Sterile," "lacking a sense of place," and "socioeconomically exclusive" are but a few of the purported qualities hurled at the communities more than one-half of all Americans now call home. Leading the charge—and capturing much media attention in the process—have been the proponents of the *new urbanism.* Whether one agrees with the planning and design principles espoused by the new urbanists, one must acknowledge that they have successfully raised our consciousness about where and how we live. Moreover, they have drawn much-needed attention to the practice of building communities.

This paper explores how some developers and planners are striving to create a stronger sense of community and place in new suburban developments. While design still plays an important role in how the residents of new communities interact with one another, many developers are turning their attention to other means of promoting the spirit of a *social* community.

Desperately Seeking Community

The first matter of importance to any discussion concerning what constitutes a strong or weak *community* is understanding what the term implies. The *Simon & Schuster Dictionary* offers a starting point: "all the people living in a particular district, city, etc."; "a group of people living together as a smaller social unit within a larger one, and having interests, work, etc., in common"; "similarity"; "likeness"; "friendly association."

At the root of what we think of as community is the existence of some type of commonality—beyond just sharing a physical space—among the members of the community. Historically, commonality was evidenced by such qualities as religious belief or ethnic heritage. Communities tended to grow around an activity or facility shared by residents, such as a church. Given the rapidly increasing diversity of suburban dwellers, less apparent forms of commonality need to be considered—common interests, values, mores, etc. This has left urban planners and community developers struggling to find ways to bring residents of new communities together in ways that promote "similarity" and foster "friendly association."

Until recently, planners and developers have tended to focus on physical design as a means of fostering community. Now, however, community developers are also looking to the programming of opportunities for social activities as a way to draw residents together. At a ULI-sponsored conference on master-planned communities held in Phoenix in January 1997, nationally renown community developer and ULI Emeritus Charles Fraser issued a call to action for community developers of master-planned communities to come together and deal with an array of emerging issues of concern to the industry. Among the concerns that Fraser raises for immediate attention are the need for uniform ordinances to deal with growth pressures at the urban fringe; cooperative efforts to retool local development regulations; implementation of programs to increase affordable housing; acknowledgment that demographics and housing demand are on a collision course with a growing lack of development sites; and, not least, ways to promote the social infrastructure of communities that will effectively bind together residents of new communities. Fraser contends that suburban developments generally have failed to provide their residents with adequate opportunity to come together as a functioning social unit.

Fraser's perspective on the concerns facing developers have been shaped by his more than 40 years of experience in developing master-planned and resort communities throughout the southeastern United States and, more recently, by his active involvement in the planning of Celebration, Florida. As a strategic consultant, Fraser worked closely with Walt Disney Imagineering in the conceptualization of what is probably the most highly anticipated new community of the last two decades. Based on the extensive research conducted during the course of preparing Celebration's master plan, Fraser became aware of the growing need to foster new towns—on a massive scale—that promote social interaction of residents. He believes that Celebration provides the prototype for establishing a healthy social and physical infrastructure for an emerging new town.

So convinced is he of the need to build better new communities, Fraser is launching a nonprofit organization to advance the cause. The American Town Design Network® will be headquartered in Celebration and draw upon a multidisciplinary team of urban development experts to help draft model ordinances, eliminate regulatory barriers, and provide training in "family and enterprise friendly new town design." Fraser hopes that this new network will bring together the many developers, planners, and academicians from around the United States who have been seeking ways to build stronger communities.

ULI Leadership Counterpoint

What needs to happen to make communities more livable? Participants in ULI's leadership roundtable discussions believe that the answer begins with a better understanding of the "glue" that binds contemporary communities together. The keys to building better communities are varied and dynamic; successful developers in the future will be those who best understand how to blend the various components of physical and social planning.

Fostering community requires an understanding of consumers. While a great deal of research has been undertaken on housing consumers, relatively little has been undertaken to understand their attitudes about the larger community in which they seek to live. As a result, many of the criticisms directed at the suburbs are based more on opinion and speculation than on rigorous research of consumer preferences. With a heightened understanding of consumer preferences, the private marketplace would be in an improved position to respond to consumers rather than just reacting to critics. Such research should extend well beyond standard demographics and delve into *psychographic* profiles of consumers.

Certainly, physical design is an important ingredient for fostering community. However, ULI's leadership does not believe it is the *only* ingredient. Although proponents of new urbanism have made significant contributions to the practice of community design, they tend to go too far in promoting the concept as a panacea for everything perceived as wrong with the suburbs. As one participant noted, "New urbanism is *not* a cure for cancer, it is a design concept that may be appealing to some percentage of the market." Proponents of new urbanism have been successful in marketing their vision to public agencies without always having the research to back up many of their claims concerning issues such as the depth and nature of the market. The danger is that new urbanism principles may become mandated by some pubic agencies without appropriate consideration of real market forces.

While new urbanism may prove to be a positive concept for at least a market niche, ULI's interests in building communities should be much broader. ULI should seek to explore the full range of ingredients contributing to a heightened sense of community and connectiveness between residents. These ingredients are not just limited to the physical plan but also include the "software side" of the community, or the "social infrastructure." Efforts by such national community developers as Walt Disney Imagineering, the Howard Hughes Corporation, and Arvida are demonstrating the importance that consumers place on the social aspects of new communities.

ULI leaders also believe that new communities cannot survive and succeed if they are developed as isolated places. Community developers should become more involved in efforts that will improve the function and economic health of the regional community. Suburban communities are most successful and prosperous when they exist in proximity to a healthy urban core. Community developers should work to ensure that new suburban communities do not emerge at the expense of the inner city. For example, suburban developers need to be involved in initiatives that will improve the quality of schools throughout the metropolitan area—not just those of the district in which a particular project is located.

To be sure, America's suburbs are not always ideal places to live. And many of the problems typically associated with inner cities are making their way to even the most remote suburban communities. ULI must be at the forefront in understanding how to confront these problems and how to build stronger communities that merge the best of physical design with maximum opportunity for social connectiveness.

This counterpoint is a summary of a roundtable discussion at the ULI Midwinter Leadership Meeting in Boca Raton, Florida, February 1997.

Is New Urbanism a Cure?

For over a decade, new urbanists have been capturing the media spotlight with a barrage of highly critical rhetoric focused squarely on the suburbs. The planning and design principles promoted by the new urbanists have been well covered in the real estate trade press (for example, see *Urban Land* series of January–August 1991) but hit the mainstream media with a May 15, 1995, *Newsweek* cover article entitled "Bye-Bye Suburban Dream: 15 Ways to Fix the Suburbs." The article's bottom line was that the suburbs are broken and new urbanism is the tool needed to fix them.

New urbanist planning principles contain many design elements that are intended to foster a heightened sense of community and opportunity for social engagement. For example, new urbanism planning places much emphasis on public and civic spaces such as village greens, pocket parks, and pedestrian ways. Houses and other buildings exhibit a much stronger orientation to streets than their more conventional suburban counterparts. These and other design practices are intended to help draw people together and open new opportunities for interaction. Essentially, they aim to get people out of their private backyards and onto their front porches where they might have a chance to bump into a neighbor. Some critics of new urbanism, however, believe that these types of design features alone are not enough to influence how people will act —or want to act.

The question of whether new urbanism is a cure for the physical and social problems plaguing the suburbs is still hotly debated. Meanwhile, proponents of new urbanism are successfully promoting their cause. In December 1996, *New Urban News* published a list of 119 "traditional neighborhood developments" that are underway in the United States. The vast majority of these new communities, however, were in either the planning stages or the earliest stages of development. Further, new urbanist-inspired communities underway to date are predominantly residential in character. New urbanists must therefore rely largely on theory rather than on experience in making their case.

One problem that has surfaced with new urbanist concepts is how to accommodate a full range of residential, employment, institutional, and commercial uses at the relatively small scale that most of these communities are conceived. Retail uses have proven especially problematic. Plans for a community-serving town center in the heart of Kentlands, located in Gaithersburg, Maryland, were delayed when a market for retailers failed to materialize. Instead, a more conventional community-level shopping center facing an arterial highway was built at the edge of the community. Although incorporating some of the architectural features that help to identify it with Kentlands, the shopping center functions in large part as any other suburban shopping center. The developers of Kentlands are still working to build a mixed-use town center within the community as originally conceived. The otherwise successful, new urbanist-styled community of Harbor Town in Memphis, Tennessee, is still awaiting development of its retail town center, which is conceived with a storefront-lined main street with residential apartments located over the stores.

Another unanswered question relates to the size of the market that would be willing to make the tradeoffs typically associated with living in a new urbanist-styled community. A 1995 survey of homebuyers conducted by San Francisco–based American LIVES, Inc., and Newport Beach, California–based Intercommunications, Inc., shed some early light on this question. It found that

- 20.8 percent of homebuyers are pro–new urbanism. This group likes the entire concept, including the higher densities, and is unhappy with the suburbs as they now exist.
- 48.4 percent of homebuyers like the concept but dislike the density. This group likes the overall concept (especially the town center) but is unwilling to accept smaller lots and reductions in the use of automobiles; this group is also unhappy with the suburbs as they now exist.
- 30.8 percent of homebuyers dislike the new urbanism. This group likes the suburbs largely as they are.

Results from the survey suggest a reasonably sized market niche for new urbanist communities. The results also point to nearly two-thirds of homebuyers who say they are dissatisfied with the suburbs as they now exist. Interestingly, however, most of those who are dissatisfied also are unwilling to give up prized suburban features such as large lots, culs-de-sac, proximity to large areas of natural open space, and easy access to freeways. Until consumers of new suburban communities are willing to make the necessary tradeoffs, they are unlikely to witness a solution to the problems they experience with conventional suburban communities. Such stubbornness on the part of suburban residents may prove to be

a difficult hurdle for proponents of new urbanism over the long term.

Another potential hurdle relates to the ability of new urbanists to build communities at the scale and speed typically associated with new suburban communities. Most new urbanist communities built to date have been relatively small and have not involved large production homebuilders. If new urbanism theory is to make a lasting impression on the suburban landscape, it must prove adaptable to larger-scale application.

A few projects on the horizon will shortly begin to test the adaptability of new urbanism to the suburban production machine. At a ULI professional development conference held in June 1996 in Reston, Virginia, developer George deGaurdiola presented plans for his 2,100-acre community of Abacoa, which is being developed near Jupiter, Florida. This community of 6,000 houses and a range of other uses will present one of the first real tests for applying new urbanist concepts to a large-scale community and production homebuilders. At Abacoa, homebuilders must comply with rigidly established "codes" to ensure that

the architectural styles and integrity of the new urbanist vision is not compromised.

New urbanists have offered up new hopes and ideas for building stronger communities—both in the suburbs and within already urbanized areas. Yet, even if their design theses prove successful in the marketplace—and a variety of lending, regulatory, and production obstacles can be overcome—there is no guarantee that the *social* aspects of the community will be significantly influenced. So far, the American experience with influencing human behavior through design has not proven promising.

Creating Third Places

In his 1989 book, *The Great Good Place*, Ray Oldenburg characterizes and ranks the three distinct "places" where people spend most of their time. *First places* are private homes; *second places* are offices or work centers; and *third places* are centers for social gathering. One could argue that community developers have been fairly successful at accommodating the first two of these place needs but have performed less successfully in pro-

The beach club and community recreation center at Rancho Santa Margarita, California, has become a popular gathering place for residents of this 5,000-acre new town. Built in an early phase of the community's development, the entire lake shore is accessible to the public and features walking and biking paths, pocket parks, playgrounds, and areas for passive recreation.

viding vital third places. Most suburban communities rely on a disjointed series of third places and lack the critical mass and range of activities to meet the full spectrum of resident needs. By default, shopping malls have come forward to fill the void, though certainly not the real need.

Large-scale community developers are turning new attention to what Oldenburg would consider to be genuine third places in the form of town centers, entertainment destinations, and public gathering places. A case in point is the Reston Town Center, which opened its first phase in 1990, some 25 years after the "new town" was launched. Reston epitomizes the practice of large-scale, suburban, planned unit development that became popular during the 1960s, in part in reaction to the disconnected residential subdivisions and strip commercial centers that flourished in the years following World War II. Reston and its design counterparts such as Columbia, Maryland, and Irvine, California, were seen as better ways to accommodate new suburban development. Accordingly, they relied heavily on the concepts of building identifiable communities and neighborhoods. Integration of residential, commercial, employment, and recreational uses was integral to Reston's master plan. Ironically, it is communities like Reston that have come under attack by new urbanists for their failure to provide for the full integration of uses and activities—at least at a meaningful human scale.

Recognizing a need to create something akin to a downtown, Reston's master developer, Mobil Land Development Corporation, initiated planning in 1982 for an 85-acre, mixed-use "urban core" within a 460-acre "town center" district. The 20-acre first phase features office buildings, a hotel, and a traditionally styled main street lined with retail shops, entertainment uses, and an array of public spaces and amenities.

Reston Town Center broke many of the suburban rules of retailing. As a result, the retail component of the center got off to a slow start and required several years of experimentation and repositioning before it became economically profitable. The entertainment and recreational components of the town center, however, experienced instant success. Large crowds are drawn to the center for special events, to eat in restaurants, to go to the cinema, to ice skate in winter, and just to gather in the outdoor public spaces during warm months. Mobil also believes that the town center has spun off benefits to the entire community of Reston by providing an urban heart, an activity hub, and a heightened perception of community.

Mizner Park in Boca Raton, Florida, is another example of the successful development of a mixed-use town center within an existing large-scale community. Mizner Park's traditional main street features a wide landscaped median that functions as a public park, storefronts facing the street, and residential and office uses above the stores. The center has become a popular location for restaurants and specialty retail shops. Recently, one end of the main street was anchored with a freestanding department store and the International Museum of Cartoon Art. Developed by Crocker & Company, Mizner Park is the product of the cooperative relationship between a private developer and the Boca Raton Community Development Agency, which successfully united business leaders, private citizens, and cultural groups behind the development concept. Today, Mizner Park is the focus of Boca Raton's downtown district and a successful community gathering place for residents as well as for tourists.

New and more ambitious town centers are emerging in large master-planned communities throughout the United States, including those in Rancho Santa Margarita, California; Valencia, California; and Summerlin, Nevada. Summerlin is an unfolding 22,500-acre, master-planned community being developed outside Las Vegas by the Howard Hughes Corporation, a subsidiary of the Rouse Company. At buildout, the community will comprise 60,000 houses, a population of 160,000, and a wide range of employment, institutional, and recreational features.

The Howard Hughes Corporation—developer of the 22,500-acre new town of Summerlin near Las Vegas—created a community mascot known to residents as Summerlin Sam. The mascot has become an effective symbol of the community spirit being nurtured by the developer and is seen frequently at community-sponsored events. To help bolster the social aspects of the community, Hughes has embarked upon an aggressive effort to program a wide range of social events and activities and forge working alliances with dozens of institutions and organizations.

The Summerlin master plan provides for a major town center organized into three zones: the 100-acre core area, which will be the heart of the downtown district; the 450- to 500-acre central business district, including and surrounding the core area; and the 1,300-acre support area, including and surrounding the CBD. The town center is intended to become the centerpiece of Summerlin as well as the retail, employment, entertainment, and cultural focus for the west side of the Las Vegas metropolitan area.

What the developers of Summerlin and other new master-planned communities have come to appreciate is the need for Oldenburg's so-called *third places* in suburbia. Real communities must consist of more than bedrooms and basic services. The human residents of these communities require access to entertainment, cultural facilities, and places to come together for social gathering. Such places are most successful when a critical mass of activities and a range of social opportunities are offered.

Shifting Focus to Social Infrastructure

Why are more Americans bowling alone? That is the question put forward by political scientist Robert Putnam in several thought-provoking writings, including "The Strange Disappearance of Civic America" (*The American Prospect*, Winter 1996). Putnam speculates that the answer lies in a general downturn in "networks, norms, and trusts . . . that enable participants to act together more effectively to pursue social objectives," or what he terms *social capital*. Further, he notes a decline of *civic engagement*, which he defines as "people's connections with the life of their communities." Putnam's research into the decline of social capital in America was the primary focus of the 1997 Annual Housing Conference sponsored in April by the Fannie Mae Foundation.

So what has brought about the decline, if not disappearance, of social capital and civic engagement in America? All evidence points to the baby boom generation and—while mobility and suburbanization were examined as root suspects—Putnam tags television as the real culprit. One might speculate that the dizzying pace of technological advances will work to draw people further into themselves and erode the human interactions we have historically associated with a healthy community.

The Marketplace at Cascades Town Center is a 215,000-square-foot destination of 34 stores and restaurants grouped into the center's three components: a 77,000-square-foot apparel and soft goods–oriented open center; an 87,000-square-foot community shopping center anchored by a major supermarket; and a one-block intimate shopping street lined with boutiques, restaurants, and cafés. The center is located on a 21.6-acre site within a 105-acre planned town center site at the heart of the master-planned community of Cascades in Loudoun County, Virginia.

The downtown district of Celebration, Florida, includes luxury apartments—many targeted to young families—within a short walking distance of the mixed-use town center. Being developed by Walt Disney Imagineering, Celebration is a 4,900-acre, master-planned community that is breaking new ground to promote community identity through a combination of physical design and social infrastructure.

Community developers are not taking the purported demise of the social compact and civic engagement lying down. Several nationally recognized development companies have organized to shift more focus to what has been called the *social infrastructure* of the community—all in an effort to bring residents together to pursue common interests and activities, thereby fostering a heightened perception of community. In the process, they have found that it is also good for business. Leading the charge in this effort, once again, is Celebration.

Members of Disney's planning and development team based Celebration's master plan on five development "cornerstones" that, on the whole, have little to do with physical design: health, education, technology, place, and community. In most of these areas, Disney assembled a team of partners in a strategic alliance to create the community and help distinguish Celebration as a special place to live. The partners included local public agencies and utilities as well as major corporations, institutions, and organizations. (For more information, see "Celebration, Florida:

Breaking New Ground," *Urban Land*, February 1997; a more detailed case study of Celebration will also appear in ULI's forthcoming book, *Trends and Innovations in Master-Planned Communities*.)

To nurture the civic infrastructure, a not-for-profit organization called the Celebration Foundation was created to function as a clearinghouse for clubs and organizations and to coordinate volunteer activities in the community. The foundation is likened to a local chamber of commerce; leadership eventually will be provided by members of the local community assisted by a full-time executive director. It is expected that the foundation will, as part of its work, promote ideas and lessons learned by the community and channel volunteer efforts to serve both Celebration and the larger community. Thus, the function of the Celebration Foundation goes well beyond that performed by a community or homeowners' association; however, other developers are structuring ways for similar community-supporting services to be fostered through a community or homeowners' association.

It is also interesting that Disney perceived advances in technology not as a threat to the social community but as an opportunity to facilitate interaction among residents. Eventually, a broadband, fiber-based optic network is planned to link the town's homes, school, health care facilities, office park, civic organizations, and retail establishments. The network will carry voice, data, and video communications for everyone in town. Other developers view technology optimistically as a way to help draw together residents of a community. Arvida has established an Internet site—known as TownTalk—for its new community of Weston located in Fort Lauderdale, Florida. The system is designed to facilitate interaction among community residents, making communication with schools, park programs, community leaders, and friends possible in a single session at the home computer.

These and other forward-thinking community developers across the United States and Canada are expanding their roles from just builders of houses and physical infrastructure to builders of a social infrastructure that can be nurtured and tended by incoming residents.

Toward a Blending of Physical and Social Infrastructure

What is the key to building stronger, identifiable communities in the years ahead? There are no quick and easy answers but experience suggests that developers will need to be attentive to both physical design and the establishment of a social infrastructure. Todd Mansfield, ULI member, former executive vice president for Walt Disney Imagineering, and leader of the development team for Celebration, offers this insight into what the future holds for developers of suburban communities:

> Traditionally, our industry has concerned itself primarily with real estate development, focusing on place but not much else. By 2010, I believe there will be a clear distinction between real estate developers and community developers. Community developers will understand that creating community is more about people than it is about real estate. At Celebration, we define community as what happens when a group of people share common practices; make decisions together; depend upon one another; and consider themselves part of something larger than the sum of their individual relationships. Our goal is to lay the foundation that will allow this community to grow. We believe that by 2010, it will not be as easy as simply being experts in environmental planning, transportation methodology, regulatory permitting, zoning, construction, and marketing. Developers will have to be adept in public health, life-long education, telecommunications, community volunteerism, and civic leadership. This makes our job as community developers much more challenging, but also substantially more interesting. By 2010, the civic infrastructure will take precedence over the physical infrastructure in the design of our master-planned communities.[1] ✳

Note

1. ULI–the Urban Land Institute, *Trends and Innovations in Master-Planned Communities* (Washington, D.C.: author, forthcoming).

Urban Change and Infill Housing Development

Diane R. Suchman

Diane R. Suchman is an urban development consultant and formerly a special assistant to the assistant secretary for policy development and research at the U.S. Department of Housing and Urban Development. She has also served as director of housing and community development research at ULI.

Over the past 30 years, the landscape of urban America has changed dramatically. As a result, one of the most important challenges facing the real estate development industry at the dawn of the 21st century is how to help redefine and revitalize many of America's central cities. Another is how to minimize the problems associated with "sprawl," including transportation, environmental, and quality-of-life concerns. One ingredient that can serve both objectives and that is essential to rebuilding central cities is the development of infill housing on vacant or underused parcels of land in inner-city neighborhoods.[1]

Any discussion of infill housing development or improvement of city neighborhoods must occur within the larger context—the physical, economic, political, and social dynamics that are shaping metropolitan areas. A number of forces are affecting all metropolitan regions and certain patterns of urban change are clear. Economic restructuring from manufacturing to service and knowledge-based industries, the global nature of modern economic activity, the dizzying pace of technological change, immigration, labor shortages, the aging of the population, environmental awareness, and changing patterns of government funding have affected the character and fortunes of all metropolitan areas.

The shift to a postindustrial, service-oriented economy has had a complex effect on patterns of urbanization. Loss of manufacturing industries in many cities has resulted in the concomitant loss of low-skill jobs that paid well. At the same time, the rise of technical and service-oriented industries has created demand for knowledge-based and service workers. Globalization of the economy has stimulated greater business mobility, efficiency, and flexibility. As a result, metropolitan areas must compete as economic regions. Rapid technological change has opened new vistas of creativity and given people and businesses more freedom of movement. Advances in communications have enabled companies to relocate their back-office functions and, in many cases, their headquarters, to suburban or even rural areas.

Economic and technological changes have also helped transform land use patterns in metropolitan areas. The most profound land use change during the last half of this century has been the suburbanization of population and jobs. As a result of this out-migration within America's 522 central cities, population density has declined by 50 percent since 1950. (The most obvious exceptions are the few cities that have experienced significant immigration.) As of 1990, almost 80 percent of the nation's population lived in the suburbs. Jobs have followed people. Today, 80 percent of new office construction is taking place in the suburbs and, in many metropolitan areas, suburbs account for a large share of office space.

Within metropolitan areas, immigrants and minorities tend to be concentrated in the urban cores. As of 1990, many central cities had "minority majorities," including Chicago (62.4 percent minority); Dallas (53.1 percent minority); Detroit (79.7 percent minority); Los Angeles (54.2 percent minority); and Washington, D.C. (73.5 percent minority).[2]

Some cities have succeeded in restructuring their economies successfully and rebuilding their downtowns and much of their inner-city areas. Others have not. The pattern of population loss is also not uniform. Of 18 central cities that lost population during the 1970s, six gained population during the 1980s. All but one of the remainder slowed the rate of population loss. Cities that serve as headquarters of corporations and related finance, insurance, and real estate (FIRE) industries tended to grow in population and employment. Port-of-entry cities such as Los Angeles, San Francisco, New York, and Miami also grew.[3] How cities have fared has depended on many factors, including the quality of local leadership, the nature of local labor markets, patterns of income and poverty, growth rates, and the types of industries present.

Urban Change and Inner-City Neighborhoods

As middle-income families have moved out of cities and into the suburbs, they have left behind impoverished residents and recent immigrants. Cities have become more racially diverse, include more young adults and elderly as a percentage of the population, and contain a greater incidence and concentration of poverty than suburban jurisdictions. As a result, racial and economic disparities between cities and suburbs have widened, and there is a spatial mismatch between jobs

ULI Leadership Counterpoint

Participants in ULI's leadership roundtables agreed that land use professionals should and do have a stake in improving conditions in central cities but that they generally do not behave as though they have such a stake. Most for-profit developers ignore potential inner-city housing markets and opportunities because of crime, poor public schools, regulatory complexity, high taxes, and the lack of community amenities and services.

Participants recognized that tax base competition among individual jurisdictions within a region has resulted in inefficient development patterns and the isolation of central cities, but they also felt that metropolitan government is not a realistic solution because suburban voters would not allow their elected officials to participate. However, the group cited several examples of successful regional cooperation for the provision of commonly needed facilities and services, including airports, transit systems, and convention facilities. Participants recommended educating outlying communities on their substantial self-interest in the vitality of the central city.

Participants agreed that if the key barriers were removed, developers would be more interested in developing infill housing in central cities, particularly in metropolitan areas where infrastructure needs and other issues have made large suburban development deals more difficult. For infill housing—especially for mixed-income populations—to be successful, the locations chosen for infill housing must be attractive places for middle-income households to live, with retail shops and services,

cultural events, recreation and entertainment (one person mentioned golf courses as a desired amenity), high-quality housing choices, and proximity to employment centers. Clearly, the two major issues that deter investment in central cities were crime and the poor quality of public education. Indeed, the ULI leaders spent considerable time discussing the impacts of these issues and how they might be addressed.

One developer said that he has spent more time and money on security issues in inner-city neighborhoods than on any other single item. Community policing efforts received high praise, as did police patrols on bicycle or horseback. Neighborhood watch programs were lauded as effective in both deterring crime and strengthening relationships among neighborhood residents. For real estate developers, perceptions that cities are dangerous (despite falling crime rates in most major cities) raise questions about whether to build gated communities, even though studies show that such communities are not really more secure.

Some were negative about the prospects for public schools, recommending the use of vouchers to make them more competitive, or even dismantling them altogether and starting over. Others emphasized that discussions on how to improve the schools must become more realistic, focusing on how to work with children who receive no parental attention or supervision, suffer from health problems or nutritional deficiencies, and demonstrate poor socialization. Still others discussed recent positive developments, including charter schools,

the introduction of computers into schools, and magnet schools—though magnet schools require busing children in and out of neighborhoods. One participant cited Los Angeles's LEARN program, through which qualifying public schools can give teachers greater independence to tailor curricula and programs to children's needs.

Participants felt city governments discourage real estate investment in inner-city neighborhoods through excessive regulation and red tape, making development in those locations unnecessarily frustrating and expensive. What is needed most is for cities to "make it easier" by reducing red tape, the overlaps in agency requirements, time delays, and the excessive standards that characterize many building codes. One way this might be done is through creation of a "super-agency" or one-stop shop that coordinates requirements for and timing of permits and approvals. In addition, to foster consensus among stakeholders and ensure predictability in the development process, the ULI developer participants noted that they preferred to work as part of a partnership that includes cities and empowered community groups. One participant indicated that he would develop in inner-city neighborhoods only if he could prenegotiate an agreement with the city that would outlast political changes.

This counterpoint is a summary of a roundtable discussion at the ULI Midwinter Leadership Meeting in Boca Raton, Florida, February 1997.

and housing and a fiscal mismatch between location of higher-income populations and revenue needs.

In addition, central cities are plagued by two issues that make them difficult places in which to live and raise children and that deter investment in the local housing market: urban school systems are perceived as ineffective (and even unsafe) warehouses of poorly educated, disadvantaged, and minority students; and distressed neighborhoods exhibit the full range of social problems associated with concentrated poverty —particularly crime, drugs, gangs, and long-term unemployment. These factors discourage middle-class households from locating in inner-city neighborhoods.

Some would say that the deterioration of city neighborhoods is both a cause and a result of low-density urban sprawl. According to Anthony Downs, "this outcome is neither accidental nor caused by the operation of free markets. Rather, it results at least in part from public policies that are hard to change because they benefit a majority of urban households."[4] He goes on to say that we have a "nationwide policy of providing low-income housing by devaluing central city neighborhoods. . . . [T]he inner city is where low-income people are supposed to be."[5]

Whatever the reasons, the fact is that many of the nation's central cities are in trouble, and this should be a matter of concern to all metropolitan area residents, regardless of where they live. The presence of blighted areas in the nation's core cities creates a sense of physical decay, economic drain, and spiritual degradation among people of the city, the region, and the nation.

Why Should Suburbanites Care about Central Cities?

Although the value of central cities is difficult to quantify, it is clear that they possess considerable value that extends beyond their jurisdictional boundaries. Cities remain the symbolic, social, and economic heart of metropolitan regions. Mention the name of a metropolitan area, and the image that springs to mind is not that of a suburban office center, but the downtown. The city is the real and symbolic center of the region—the physical embodiment of the city's history, character, and business reputation. It can be a source of civic pride—or embarrassment—to all area citizens.

Within the historic central city stand the architecturally distinctive buildings, monuments, plazas, and streetscapes that evoke the city's unique history and character. Cities often contain government complexes, great universities, convention centers, museums, hospital centers, libraries, retail districts, zoos, performing arts centers, research institutions, and sports facilities that serve the entire region, offering a wide range of cultural events, civic activities, educational opportunities, entertainment, and recreational opportunities.

Viable and attractive central cities also use these elements to generate considerable tourism activity that in many cases is a major element in the regional economy. Cities such as New York, Boston, Washington, D.C., Miami, Chicago, Las Vegas, San Francisco, Los Angeles, New Orleans, and Seattle —to name a few—all have central-city economies that thrive on tourism. Suburbs, on the other hand, are seldom major tourist destinations. When severe problems develop in a central city or it receives negative publicity, tourism—as well as the regional economy—suffers. Any urban area that declines to the point where it is perceived as unsafe or unattractive for tourism will lose this business, and the considerable regional economic benefits that go with it will be lost as well.

Central cities tend to perform several other specific functions well. They provide the location of choice for activities that benefit from face-to-face communication among a city's public and private leaders. The high density of cities enables decision makers to gather and share information, skills, products, and services. As a result, notes one urban scholar, "many of the great innovations of the U.S. economy have been incubated in the nation's cities."[6]

Some observers have argued that advancing technology has made face-to-face contact less important, yet electronic communication "cannot be randomized or accidental in the same way as meetings at offices, restaurants, churches, or just off the street. Nor can electronic meetings convey the same completeness of meaning as face-to-face contacts. . . . [A]nd, electronic contacts cannot be entirely entrusted with the confidential communication so important in politics and government affairs."[7] In addition, cities have "unique agglomeration economies that define an important and specialized role for the central city and the region. . . . [D]ense urban environments can lead to unexpected combinations of seemingly unrelated ideas that may provide important leaps forward in knowledge."[8]

Moreover, a recent survey of residents of the 100 largest American cities revealed that among residents of the suburbs, half included at least one family member who worked in the central city; 67 percent depended on the central city for major medical care; and 43 percent had a family member attending (or planning to attend) a central-city-based institution of higher learning.[9]

Central cities are also important to the regional economy and its ability to compete in the global marketplace. Because of their location and critical mass, central cities are fertile environments for firms and individuals that offer a high degree of expertise in specialized services. Companies located in suburban jurisdictions often depend on central-city suppliers for various corporate services, and many highly paid suburbanites work in the central city. In fact, wages for central-city jobs are, on average, 20 percent higher than suburban jobs, though many of these high-paying jobs are held by suburbanites.[10]

A number of studies indicate that the fortunes of central cities and their suburbs move in concert.[11] Where cities tend to be strong and productive, suburban prosperity is greater. There is a direct correlation between city-suburban disparity and overall regional economic growth. Where disparities are great, economic growth is slower. And population change in central cities is related to suburban population growth; cities with high rates of population loss have declining or slower-growing suburbs. In short, cities (and suburbs) have come to be recognized as parts of a larger, regional economic unit that cannot be easily defined or divided along traditional jurisdictional lines.[12]

From a physical standpoint, central cities represent substantial public and private investment in the built environment (infrastructure, buildings, etc.). Allowing that physical investment to deteriorate, and with it the social fabric of the community, is wasteful and threatens not only the quality of life of city residents, but also the vitality of nearby areas—where such deterioration can easily spread—and ultimately the entire region.

Jonathan Barnett lists three reasons why residents of suburbs should care about what happens in cities: logic (federal and local government actions largely cause inner-city conditions so metropolitan-scale solutions are needed and metropolitanwide sharing of responsibility is appropriate); idealism (poverty and racism are the root causes of central-city decline, and both the causes and the result are inconsistent with the ideals of democracy and capitalism, the teach-

ings of religion, and the voice of conscience); and enlightened self-interest or fear (if we don't do something about the causes of inner-city conditions, the problems will spread and eventually affect a much broader area).[13]

Rebuilding the City

Re-creating vibrant central cities will require a multipronged strategy that includes redefining the functions of the metropolitan core consistent with global economic realities, metropolitan land use patterns, and continuing advances in technology. It will involve building a new economic base consistent with those redefined functions, ensuring access from within and beyond the city core, finding productive ways to reuse obsolete buildings (especially by rehabilitating architecturally and historically significant structures), and creating environments that invite people to gather. And it will involve making cities more livable by revitalizing and attracting a more diverse population to the deteriorated older neighborhoods near the central business district and inner suburbs.

In tackling the revitalization of urban neighborhoods, at least two economic and social agendas —both important to the larger community of Americans—are involved: rebuilding inner-city neighborhoods because they are important to the vitality of the downtown and the downtown is important to the vitality of the region; and revitalizing inner-city neighborhoods to enable existing residents to live in decent homes and neighborhoods and become productive, self-sufficient members of society.

Michael Porter of Harvard University advocates revitalizing inner-city neighborhoods by exploiting their competitive advantages (strategic location, local market demand, and integration with regional clusters and human resources) to create

City Life is a medium-density, mixed-income, infill development on a 40,000-square-foot site in an inner-city neighborhood near downtown Portland, Oregon.

an economic base that will generate jobs and incomes, rather than providing assistance to households or making physical improvements.[14] Most observers recommend a mixed approach that includes encouraging economic development, improving neighborhoods, increasing and economically diversifying the residential population by expanding housing opportunities, and providing various kinds of assistance to needy families—including assistance in moving elsewhere.

Creating new housing opportunities in central cities can be achieved through a number of different approaches used in combination. Many cities, such as Milwaukee, Chicago, and Washington, D.C., have aggressively promoted downtown housing by encouraging construction of luxury rental apartments and condominiums in the downtown area. In some cities, such as New York and Denver, existing vacant, underused, or obsolete buildings are being transformed into rental apartments. Other cities, such as Memphis and Pittsburgh, contain large tracts of underused land near the downtown core that are being developed as new communities. In other areas, such as Atlanta and St. Louis, distressed public housing developments are being demolished or rehabilitated and rebuilt as mixed-income communities.[15] Another approach is to help revitalize inner-city neighborhoods through privately developed infill housing projects.

Developing Infill Housing

The development of infill housing projects by private developers is an important link in the chain of activities needed to strengthen cities and rebuild inner-city neighborhoods. (Infill housing here refers to individual housing projects rather than large-scale clearing and revitalization of neighborhoods.) Infill housing can serve a potential market niche while enhancing the residential character of inner-city neighborhoods, but to be sustainable and to affect the future viability of central cities, infill development must be part of a larger, more comprehensive effort to revitalize central cities and improve the life chances of their residents.[16]

Development of infill sites in established city neighborhoods can provide many public benefits. Most obviously, such development can help improve existing city neighborhoods and the environments in which existing residents live. By providing needed new rental and homeownership housing choices, it can help retain (or attract back to the city) much-valued middle-income taxpayers. A larger, more economically

diverse resident population in the city will, in turn, promote additional investment by creating demand for more goods and services. Infill development can enable local governments to privatize their inventories of publicly owned properties and put vacant land and buildings back on the tax rolls. Development of infill parcels can also help rebuild the city fabric, eliminate existing and potential neighborhood eyesores, and fuel additional investment and economic activity within the community. Particularly when it involves rehabilitation of older buildings, infill development can help preserve the existing housing stock and historic structures and help retain the community's character and cultural heritage.

In addition, as part of a regional strategy to accommodate population growth, wise reuse of infill parcels can minimize the consumption of agricultural land and other open space at the urban fringe and reduce long commutes, automobile use, and fuel consumption by creating housing close to the central city and to public transit.

In considering whether to participate in housing development in inner-city areas, a developer must of course consider the nature and level of market demand for housing in city locations. The diverse pool of downtown workers—especially service sector workers employed by large, downtown firms and institutions—who would prefer to live near their work are clearly one category of demand, as are committed urbanites and "urban pioneers," current city residents seeking homeownership opportunities, and former city residents who would return to their old neighborhoods if better housing were available. Because schools are an issue and many central cities have troubled school systems, single people, childless couples, empty nesters, gay couples without children, affluent families with children in private school, and the elderly all represent potential market segments.

The strength of potential demand for city housing will vary according to local conditions. Cities with strong economies, especially central-city office markets, are clearly more attractive infill housing markets than those with weak economies. High-growth regions with suburban jurisdictions that restrict new housing through exclusionary zoning, high development fees, or growth boundaries create opportunities for infill developers as well. Cities with large tracts of available land or attractive, underused historic buildings offer opportunities for unique and creative infill developments. And in cities experiencing growing immigrant populations, developers will find ready markets for housing that is designed and priced to meet the specific demands and buying power of the incoming groups.

Often the most appropriate type of housing for city locations is mixed-income housing.[17] Historically, cities have always contained naturally occurring mixed-income communities, and recreation of that model in new or rehabilitated housing is not only healthy for neighborhoods but also can be an effective vehicle for attracting a more economically diverse population. Experience in marketing inner-city, mixed-income housing projects to households within the targeted income bands has been generally successful. Because portions of mixed-income developments are subsidized, the income mix for a particular project will depend on need or market demand as well as on the requirements of the subsidies used.

With the potential market and public benefits of developing housing in the inner city, why then has the development community not been eager to redevelop sites in these well-located neighborhoods? Developing within existing city environments is more challenging and less predictable than developing raw suburban land. Though the infrastructure is already in place, it may need to be repaired, upgraded, or modernized. Where little comparable development has occurred in recent years, the market has not been tested. City land may have been contaminated by a previous use, and older buildings may contain unacceptable levels of asbestos, radon, or lead. In addition, development costs tend to be higher in central cities because cities are typically highly regulated environments; and if federal funds are used, Davis-Bacon wage requirements will apply. There may also be problems with high land costs or acquisition and assembly. Moreover, distressed neighborhoods can be difficult development environments and can impose substantial marketing problems. In addition to image problems, existing residents, fearing gentrification and displacement, may resist change, and local residents and politicians may fear that an influx of newcomers will mean loss of political power.

On the other hand, in cities where city government leadership is supportive, infill housing developers can reasonably expect a great deal of help. There are a number of ways that cities can encourage infill development. They can establish a planning and regulatory framework that removes barriers and encourages infill housing development by, for example, targeting areas where infill development should occur and will be supported; collaborating with other city agencies

to facilitate development; streamlining the development process; and ensuring the regulatory flexibility needed to create higher-density, mixed-use, or other locally appropriate development. They can make public investments and infrastructure improvements in targeted communities, provide buildable land or assist developers with land assembly and acquisition, remediate environmental problems, help gain community acceptance for infill projects, offer various kinds of incentives and financial assistance, and provide various other forms of assistance—from initiating demonstration projects to providing an inventory of potential sites to participating in development partnerships.[18] And they can comprehensively address the various physical, social, and economic needs of neighborhoods designated for infill development.

Infill housing developments should be large enough to create a critical mass that will herald significant positive change in the neighborhood. They should be located near strong, viable areas or institutions rather than in the center of a distressed area. Project design should reflect the

Genesis Apartments at Union Square in New York is a 12-story residential complex that provides low-cost, permanent housing for the homeless and low-income population. The site had been a battleground between proponents of luxury housing and advocates for moderate-income housing, but was eventually acquired by Housing Enterprise for the Less Privileged (HELP), founded by Andrew Cuomo in 1986.

Gables Town Lake is a luxury gated multi-family community that includes 256 rental units on 12 acres. The infill site is located 1.5 miles from the heart of downtown Austin on land leased from the University of Texas.

neighborhood context and should be compatibly integrated into the surrounding community in terms of architectural style, street patterns, and scale. The development has to be affordable and "part of an area large enough, and complete enough, to be clearly distinguishable from deteriorated inner-city districts."[19] It must be realistic in terms of number of units, density, and quality, and the city and community must support development of the project.

As a general rule, financing for infill housing developments, particularly those that are targeted to a mix of incomes, cannot be accomplished successfully by relying on conventional financing models and funding sources. In addition to the types of assistance that can be expected from the city as noted before, financing must be pieced together by using a number of public and private sources. Thus, the financing for each project will differ and will depend on the nature of the project, the types and levels of funding sources available at the state and local levels, and the degree of public commitment to the project's goals. Individual developers who choose this market niche tend to rely repeatedly on their preferred types of financing sources and structures.

Some of the financing sources that are used to develop infill housing include pass-through federal Community Development Block Grant and Home Investment and Affordable Housing Partnership Act (HOME) funds, state and local taxable or tax-exempt bonds, tax-increment financing (TIF) from the city, grants or loans (often soft seconds) from the city or the state housing finance agency, and predevelopment funds from the city or from foundations. In mixed-income

projects, federal low-income housing tax credits, used alone or in combination with historic rehabilitation tax credits, often provide the source of equity financing for the income-restricted units. In addition, when the target market includes low-income households, the developer may want to consider obtaining HUD Section 8 project-based subsidies and certificates.

The Larger Picture

City governments can encourage neighborhood revitalization and infill housing development projects in numerous ways. But without regional strategies to manage regional development and economic growth, efforts at inner-city revitalization will be overwhelmed by collective public policies that encourage out-migration. A strong market for infill development will not exist if there is ample, cheap, serviced land readily available in the suburbs.

There is a long list of ways that federal, state, and local governments can encourage revitalization of the nation's central cities, should they choose to do so. For example, federal policies can offer incentives to encourage metropolitan reorganization, slow sprawl by amending the requirements imposed on infrastructure grants, modify other anticity federal policies, and broaden efforts to fix public housing by lowering the density and geographic concentration of projects and transforming distressed public housing developments into mixed-income communities.

In addition, the federal government can encourage private capital investment in inner-city neighborhoods by permanently extending the low-income housing tax credit, which has largely been used to fund central-city projects;[20] by expanding the Empowerment Zones/Enterprise Communities program; and by continuing the Community Reinvestment Act requirements. Strict federal enforcement of fair housing and fair lending laws can help ensure equal access to housing for people of all races and ethnicity. Some other options include revenue sharing to temper the fiscal imbalance between cities and suburbs and strengthening the Intermodal Surface Transportation Efficiency Act of 1991 (ISTEA) to promote regionwide planning and wise use of regional transportation resources.

States can support central cities by unifying local governments, authorizing annexation, limiting the formation of new municipalities, and promoting regional partnerships.[21] States also can impose affordable housing requirements, limit exclusionary land use practices by individual jurisdictions, promote regional economic development, and encourage local governments to participate in areawide growth management strategies.

For their part, suburban jurisdictions must recognize that the vitality—or lack of vitality—in the central city has regional implications and will require regional solutions. To address these problems and needs, suburban jurisdictions must actively participate in areawide growth management approaches, regional economic development efforts, revenue-sharing arrangements, and metropolitan housing strategies.

Change in residential neighborhoods is inevitable as structures age and new locations become fashionable places to live. But the distress evident in many of America's cities today is not simply the result of stylistic obsolescence. It is the result of powerful economic and market forces and of public actions to encourage suburbanization and to contain poor and minority households within central cities.

Just as America's metropolitan areas have undergone profound transformations in the last half of this century, so change will continue. The nature of that change will depend on many forces—demographic, economic, and social demands—but also on the kinds of decisions made by today's generation of public officials and real estate professionals. Such decisions will affect not only the fortunes of the central city, but also will determine the nature of growth and development for the entire metropolitan area. ✳

Notes

1. For discussion of infill housing development by for-profit developers, see Diane R. Suchman, "Infill Housing: Opportunities and Strategies for Inner-City Neighborhoods," ULI Research Working Paper #653, June 1996.

2. Eli Ginzberg, "The Changing Urban Scene: 1960–90 and Beyond," in Henry Cisneros, ed., *Interwoven Destinies*, The Eighty-Second American Assembly, Columbia University, April 15–18, 1993 (participants' edition), pp. 6–7.

3. William H. Frey and Elaine L. Fielding, "Changing Urban Populations: Regional Restructuring, Racial Polarization, and Poverty Concentration," *Cityscape*, June 1995, p. 14.

4. Katherine L. Bradbury, Anthony Downs, and Kenneth Small, *Urban Decline and the Future of American Cities* (Washington, D.C.: The Brookings Institution, 1982), p.177.

5. Anthony Downs, *New Visions for Metropolitan America* (Washington, D.C.: The Brookings Institu-

tion; and Cambridge, Mass.: Lincoln Institute of Land Policy, 1994), p. 69.

6. Franklin J. James, "Urban Economics: Trends, Forces, and Implications for the President's National Urban Policy," *Cityscape*, June 1995, p. 67.

7. Downs, *New Visions for Metropolitan America*, p. 52.

8. Keith R. Ihlanfeldt, "The Importance of the Central City to the Regional and National Economy: A Review of the Empirical Evidence," *Cityscape*, June 1995, p. 126.

9. Elliot Sclar and Walter Hook, "The Importance of Cities to the National Economy," in Henry Cisneros, ed., *Interwoven Destinies*, The Eighty-Second American Assemby, Columbia University, April 15–18, 1993 (participants' edition), p. 3.

10. Ibid., p. 2.

11. For example, according to Larry C. Ledebur and William R. Barnes, *All In It Together: Cities, Suburbs, and Economic Regions* (Washington, D.C.: National League of Cities, 1993), an analysis of 78 metropolitan areas showed that changes in city and suburban incomes over a ten-year period tended to be directly related.

12. William R. Barnes and Larry C. Ledebur, "Local Economies: The U.S. Common Market of Local Economic Regions," *The Regionalist*, Spring 1995, p. 20.

13. Jonathan Barnett, *The Fractured Metropolis* (New York: Harper Collins, 1995), p. 125.

14. Michael E. Porter, "The Competitive Advantage of the Inner-City," *Harvard Business Review*, May–June 1995.

15. See Richard W. Huffman, "A New Look at Inner-City Housing," *Urban Land*, January 1997; Lew Sichelman, "Converting Offices to Homes," *Urban Land*, January 1997; and Diane R. Suchman, "Transforming Public Housing Developments into Mixed-Income Communities," ULI Working Paper #653, June 1996.

16. For more information on comprehensive strategies for neighborhood revitalization, see Diane R. Suchman, *Revitalizing Low-Income Neighborhoods* (Washington, D.C.: ULI–the Urban Land Institute, 1993).

17. See Diane R. Suchman, "Mixed-Income Housing," ULI Research Working Paper #641, March 1995.

18. For more information, including case studies, on how cities can encourage infill housing development, see Nancy Bragado, Judy Corbett, and Sharon Sprowls, "Building Livable Communities: A Policy-Maker's Guide to Infill Development," Center for Livable Communities/Local Government Commission, 1995.

19. Barnett, *The Fractured Metropolis*, p. 140.

20. According to HUD's Office of Policy Development and Research, 53.6 percent of LIHTC units are located in central cities; 26.6 percent in the suburbs; and 19.8 percent in nonmetropolitan areas.

21. David Rusk, *Cities without Suburbs* (Washington, D.C.: The Woodrow Wilson Center Press, 1995), pp. 93–105.

Obsolescence to Opportunity: Adapting Outmoded Buildings For New Uses

Jo Allen Gause

Jo Allen Gause is director of office/industrial development research at ULI and is the author of the ULI book *New Uses for Obsolete Buildings,* published in 1996. She is currently directing the research and writing of the second edition of ULI's *Office Development Handbook.*

Despite obvious and continuing problems, central cities today are exhibiting some unmistakably stronger vital signs. Thanks to an expanding economy and little new construction in recent years, occupancies in top-quality downtown office buildings are up to levels not seen since before the bottom fell out of the commercial real estate market in the early 1990s. Some metropolitan areas—Seattle, Salt Lake City, Boston, and Minneapolis, to name a few—have downtown office markets as strong as, or stronger than, their suburbs. And in 1996, New York City saw more new job growth than its surrounding suburbs and edge cities for the first time since 1980.

Yet, this good news does not necessarily signal an urban renaissance. Not far from the mostly new and occupied high-end office buildings are the older business and industrial districts that are struggling with Class C buildings, dilapidated industrial facilities, and vacant lots. In the last several years, a growing inventory of underused buildings has tarnished the image of our urban cores. These include not only old buildings, but also 1960s glass skyscrapers, medium-sized concrete office boxes, abandoned warehouses, and contaminated manufacturing plants. Though many of these buildings are structurally sound, they have become functionally obsolete; that is, they are no longer able to meet the needs of the tenant base for which they were designed.

The future of the nation's central cities is in part tied to our ability to bring life back to obsolete buildings by reusing them for alternative uses. Success depends on understanding the conditions that drive the opportunities for converting existing structures to economically feasible new uses and on understanding the outlook for future opportunities.

A Glut of Obsolete Commercial Buildings

In the late 1980s and early 1990s, overbuilding, a weak economy, and a soft real estate market allowed tenants in older office buildings to move to newer Class A space at lease rates comparable to what they had been paying. These market conditions—coupled with both rapidly advancing standards for communication and information technology and modifications in building codes and safety requirements—have resulted in a large number of buildings filtering down into the Class B and C segments of the market in recent years. While some well-located older buildings can be upgraded economically to compete at higher rent levels, a significant portion of the buildings in the lower-quality range are likely to languish indefinitely.

Unfortunately, there is no reliable measure of the amount of truly obsolete office space. Class C office space data, which are available only for some metropolitan areas and their central business districts (CBDs), for example, include buildings at the low end of the quality spectrum but exclude properties taken completely out of service.

Nevertheless, the amount of vacant Class C office space alone is staggering in some markets. In downtown Dallas, for example, Class C vacancies rose from 33 percent in 1987 to 70 percent in 1996. Similarly, in downtown Chicago, Class C vacancies increased from 12 percent in 1989 to 26 percent in 1996, representing about 6 million square feet of space. With more than 11 million square feet of Class A and B space still vacant in downtown Chicago, it is reasonable to assume that the office life cycle is completed for much of the Class C inventory.

Like the office market sector, the industrial market is recovering from several years of soft market conditions. Overall demand for space in well-located modern warehouses, light manufacturing facilities, and research and development buildings is exceptionally strong today. The picture is not as bright, however, for older industrial buildings in central cities. Many of the extensive industrial areas within central cities that were developed more than 20 years ago are facing softening demand and obsolescence as the market for industrial space continues to shift from central cities to suburban sites (about two-thirds of the industrial property stock is located in suburban locations), and as new production and technologies and distribution systems force a shift to new plants and warehouses.

Adding to the challenge of finding productive new uses for surplus buildings is the fact that the structures often are concentrated in the midst of declining business and industrial districts. These commercial areas typically suffer from a poor image and lack a mix of other uses such as retail and residential, making them more difficult to adapt to new markets. On the plus side, however, most deteriorated commercial districts are not, strictly speaking, isolated ghost towns. Instead, they have the advantage of being part of a larger urban environment, one with dense mixed-use patterns of development and a dynamic ability to adapt to changing markets. Once run-down abandoned industrial areas like SoHo and TriBeCa in New York City, San Francisco's SOMA district, and the warehouse district near downtown Dallas are now fashionable arts, shopping, entertainment, and living districts.

Ingredients for Success

Fifteen years ago, most adaptive use projects were oriented toward preserving historically and architecturally significant buildings. Today,

ULI Leadership Counterpoint

The ULI leadership agreed that obsolete buildings jeopardize the future viability of downtowns in large cities and small towns alike. Housing was seen as one of the most feasible new uses for underused buildings such as aging warehouse facilities and obsolete office buildings. And bringing in new housing, particularly market-rate units, is seen as a key first step in revitalizing dying downtowns. Along with residents come retail and service establishments, restaurants, and a mix of other uses that foster urban vitality.

Roundtable participants also noted that reuse opportunities are shaped by local market demand; many cities and towns, most in fact, have not demonstrated demand for downtown housing. The tough call for the developer then is to determine if the seemingly slack demand is due largely to a lack of supply. Roundtable participants from cities like Los Angeles, where there is little demand for downtown housing, cite other strong reuse opportunities— such as cultural and entertainment-oriented uses—for older buildings.

In addition to market acceptability, the leadership identified three other obstacles that stand in the way of market-driven reuse: municipal ordinances and codes

that do not permit new uses or requirements that make conversion prohibitively expensive; lack of retail and services to support new uses; and reusing buildings with exceedingly large floorplates whose depth makes it difficult to bring in natural light. With some encouraging exceptions, participants do not see much flexibility on the part of local governments.

Roundtable participants suggested some strategies for expanding the opportunities to convert obsolete buildings to feasible new uses.

• To spread the risk of pioneering in a deteriorated area and to reach more quickly the critical mass needed to attract retail and support services, three or four developers can form a coalition, each developing 150 or so housing units, using different architects to create different floorplans. Although bringing on this many units at one time flies in the face of conventional wisdom, participants say the approach has worked in areas where there is demand for but scarce supply of central-city housing.
• Municipalities should consider selling city-owned underused land and improvements at low prices to developers or investors willing to undertake redevelop-

ment. From the city's perspective, it is better to sell low-revenue-producing properties cheaply and thus expand the tax base.
• City governments can effectively encourage the private sector to redevelop buildings with incentives such as property tax abatements, financing assistance, and modified zoning and building code regulations. It is important for private sector interests to convince elected officials that such measures would benefit the city, as the impetus for change rarely comes from inside the municipal bureaucracy.
• To overcome anticipated government resistance to a reuse project, developers should build a groundswell of support from the community before taking the project through the approval process.

It takes intense involvement and collaboration between the public and private sectors to revitalize central cities. The leadership agreed that ULI should create forums in which ideas and successful strategies are shared and made widely available.

This counterpoint is a summary of a roundtable discussion at the ULI Midwinter Leadership Meeting in Boca Raton, Florida, February 1997.

reused buildings are just as likely to be public eyesores as architecturally significant structures, and redevelopment may involve a substantial redesign of both the exterior and interior.

Like all real estate development, successful adaptive use development is part art and part science. Each potential building conversion comes with a unique package of structural, market, regulatory, and financing variables that affect development feasibility and ultimately determine whether the project sponsor's objectives will be met. Part of the art is in recognizing the advantages and disadvantages inherent in a situation and knowing when the advantages add up to a feasible opportunity. Some strategies and bonuses that can help turn obsolete buildings into "opportunity packages" are discussed below.

Understanding the Market

The oversupply of inexpensive surplus buildings has created a greater potential for adaptive use than ever before, but availability alone does not create demand. Like conventional development, adaptive use must respond to market demand; thus, such projects should be sought out based on strong locational and market fundamentals.

Bruce M. Hoch, whose firm Development Concepts Group in West Orange, New Jersey, helps identify disposition and adaptive use opportunities for underused buildings, advises that when evaluating an existing property's reuse potential, a developer should "look first to the local market demand, not to the structure itself, to suggest viable new uses." In exploring the marketability of alternative uses, Hoch suggests that the developer conduct a two-step litmus test that asks the following questions:

• Would market opportunity warrant the construction of a new facility at the existing location if the site were vacant?
• Can the existing facility be economically modified to accommodate market demand?

The highest and best use for a building will emerge by comparing the income and cost potentials of a few alternative uses that could be supported by market demand. Once the developer is convinced that a potential reuse has economic merit, even more detailed analyses of the structure itself should be undertaken to identify the potential risks in design and construction and to fine-tune cost and timing estimates. In market-based building reuse, it is imperative that the developer commit the time and money upfront to understand both the local market demand for a poten-

tial new use and the costs of fitting the proposed program to the existing building layout.

Price, Timing, and Zoning Advantages

By definition, obsolete structures are not worth much. When competition has bid down building rents to levels that barely cover operating costs— and with high vacancy rates expected to continue indefinitely—the value of those assets generally is near zero.

The combination of low acquisition prices and reusable building infrastructure can mean that redeveloping an existing building is less expensive than constructing the same-quality product from the ground up. Stated another way, without bargain purchase prices, it is rarely feasible to redevelop an existing building. Because idle assets still drain money from owners in the form of maintenance costs and real estate taxes, building owners often are eager to sell their properties, even at rock-bottom prices.

For example, when General Motors closed an old 3 million-square-foot automobile assembly plant in St. Louis in 1987, the company obtained an estimate of more than $15 million for demolition and removal of debris. At that price, GM was willing to consider other alternatives for its "white elephant," and developer Harold Clark, chair of Clark Properties, offered one. Clark convinced GM to sell the property to him for $500,000, with GM providing about $2 million to pay for asbestos removal and other environmental remediation measures. By fall 1996, Clark had redeveloped the former plant into a first-class, campus-style, multiuser warehouse, distribution, and processing complex, known as Union Seventy Center.

Sometimes the primary motivation for reusing an existing structure is that it presents a golden opportunity to open a project quickly, allowing the developer to respond nimbly to the market. With the basic structure in place, construction times can be much shorter than starting from scratch. Further, if the zoning that governs an existing building allows a proposed new use "by right," obtaining the necessary approvals and permitting for reuse can be accomplished much more quickly and less expensively than new development, and without the risk of public opposition.

Zoning ordinances can present other attractive opportunities for reuse, as when an existing building has been "grandfathered" under more favorable zoning provisions. Such was the case with the Trump International Hotel and Tower (TIHT), a luxury hotel and condominium building that has been recast from a functionally obsolete high-rise office tower on Manhattan's Columbus Circle. When the former Gulf & Western Building was constructed in 1968, a zoning variance allowed its height to reach 52 stories. Under New York City's current zoning, a newly constructed building on this same site would be restricted to a maximum height of 29 stories. By reusing the office tower's steel frame and completely redeveloping the building's exterior and interior, the developers of TIHT were able to take advantage of the obsolete building's nonconforming height and setback standards, which would never gain approval today.

The Appeal of Older Buildings

Another advantage that adaptive use offers is the possibility of developing an alternative product that can be created only from older buildings. Many adaptive use developers are not trying simply to reproduce existing products at lower prices but rather to develop and deliver a unique product that serves a niche for unique products.

It is not only historically and architecturally significant buildings that can be appreciated for their distinctive characteristics. Despite their unattractive exteriors and layers of latter-day renovations, many older commercial buildings have "good bones" that, when allowed to show through, can create desirable space for a variety of new uses. Building materials that in their day were considered "unfinished" and were covered up, for example, are highly prized today and are often left exposed: high ceilings, an abundance of large windows, wood columns and beams, brick walls, old concrete floors, and so on—all with the patina of age that cannot be reproduced.

Rick Holliday, whose company McKenzie, Rose & Holliday Development Company in San Francisco has turned several vacant warehouse and light industrial buildings into market-rate for-sale live/work lofts in San Francisco's SOMA district, recalls that he rejected at least 150 structures before taking on his first loft conversion in 1988. Since that project, which sold out in one weekend, Holliday has learned to make a rapid assessment of the structural attributes of an old building that make such a building well suited to the emerging lifestyle of home offices and electronic commutes: load-bearing exterior walls with internal column and beam structural systems; well-proportioned, well-placed windows on two or three sides of the building; generous ceiling heights; and use of brick and timber. Holliday always incorporates

unusual but not necessarily expensive finishes that set his lofts apart from others. He has hired local artists to paint benches and mosaic tiles, and has used such elements as copper inlays, polished concrete floors and sinks, and floor-to-ceiling bookcases.

Public Incentives

During the 1960s and 1970s, well-funded federal redevelopment programs supported hundreds of adaptive use projects in central cities while historic tax credits provided the impetus during much of the 1980s. But as more urban residents and employers moved to the suburbs, political support for urban revitalization waned. By the end of the 1980s, the federal government had largely backed away from funding urban redevelopment programs, shifting the responsibility to local governments.

State and local governments recognize that redevelopment is the key to renewing central cities, but given the realities of the day—reduced federal funding and increasing demands on already

Walt Disney Imagineering used a derelict warehouse in Glendale, California, to create an open and stimulating office environment for its theme park designers.

strained budgets—public funds to subsidize private investment are limited. Rather than expecting governments to solve all the problems that besiege central cities, a potentially more effective model that seems to be emerging combines the efforts and resources of private economic and community development organizations with local governments.

Though much reduced from earlier levels, public incentives can still help boost the economic feasibility of market-based adaptive use projects. The two most widely used federal programs designed to aid community revitalization are the rehabilitation tax credit, which provides a federal income tax credit equivalent to 20 percent of the qualified construction costs incurred in rehabilitating historic income-producing properties, and the low-income housing tax credit (LIHTC), which offers a dollar-for-dollar credit against federal income tax for construction costs related to mixed- or low-income housing units.

State and local incentives aimed at encouraging the private sector to redevelop underused buildings have shifted away from the direct cash subsidies of former federal urban renewal programs to tax abatements and other cost reductions that enhance economic feasibility. Types of incentives frequently include

• real estate tax abatements for the improved value of commercial and industrial properties that are converted to new uses, often specifically to residential use;

• tax abatements and credits for rehabilitating historic structures;
• changes in zoning ordinances and building codes that remove some of the risks and costs of rehabilitating older buildings for new uses;
• low-interest financing assistance through the sale of tax-exempt bonds by the city or a redevelopment authority, or committing state and federal funding or other grant resources to this effort; and
• assistance with environmental cleanup and infrastructure improvements.

One example of municipal action taken to spur the transformation of a blighted office district into a vibrant mixed-use environment is New York City's Lower Manhattan Plan, proposed by the Giuliani administration and signed into law in October 1995. Lower Manhattan, the traditional financial and insurance district of New York City, has a serious oversupply of obsolete office space. According to Torto Wheaton Research, lower Manhattan accounts for about 10 million square feet of vacant Class B and C office space. Much of this space is in pre–World War II buildings that have become too technologically and structurally obsolete to accommodate corporate tenants ever again.

Despite the surplus of commercial space in lower Manhattan, the demand for housing in the city has never been stronger; the overall vacancy rate for market-rate rental units hovers at around 1 percent. The Lower Manhattan Plan's incentive package is aimed at redeveloping Manhattan's outdated downtown financial district to meet some of that demand. The plan includes a twofold program of tax benefits and zoning changes designed to encourage the private sector to convert commercial buildings to residential and mixed uses (primarily apartments on the upper floors of buildings and retail and office space on the ground floor). Tax benefits include a 14-year phased tax abatement for mixed-use conversions and commercial renovations. Zoning changes intended to enhance the economic feasibility of converting buildings to housing include reduced minimum average floor area per dwelling unit, which enables greater density, and home offices in apartment units with up to three employees. The city's incentive package and the efforts of the Alliance for Downtown New York, a business improvement district, are having a positive effect. As of mid-year 1996, the redevelopment and conversion of approximately ten commercial buildings of varying sizes to residential use was underway, with another dozen conversions in planning.

The former Homer Savings Bank building in Milwaukee is now Historic King Place; the development effort involved the conversion of an office building to a multiuse structure that includes 41 affordable housing units and commercial space on the first floor.

Some cities are trying to facilitate redevelopment by eliminating zoning and building code regulations that impede conversion of downtown buildings to new uses. Building codes can be modified to allow flexibility in the application of regulations that govern the renovation of existing structures for new uses, such as assigning safety scores to a series of life safety features like sprinkler systems and maximum distances between fire exits. This allows buildings to receive a passing grade by achieving some but not all areas of compliance with the building code, thereby making redevelopment significantly less expensive while still ensuring a building's safety.

Business Improvement Districts

Public incentives alone will not induce developers to find alternative uses for surplus buildings when structures are located in crime-ridden, deteriorating urban neighborhoods where no one wants to live or work. To take the risk of pioneering in transitional neighborhoods, developers need to see at least the possibility of an emerging urban community. During the last decade, business improvement districts (BIDs) have proved to be a major force in helping to reestablish battered commercial districts as healthy places to live, work, visit, and invest in, thus opening up redevelopment opportunities.

BIDs are mechanisms that allow the downtown community itself—businesses, property owners, and residents—to band together to finance and manage services and physical improvements within designated areas to enhance economic vitality. BIDs typically provide a range of services that supplement municipal services such as security, garbage removal, and maintenance and that deliver nongovernmental services such as marketing, business attractions, and advocacy of business policy positions. In addition, they may fund improvements to streets, sidewalks, signage, lighting, trash receptacles, landscaping, and other elements of the physical environment. Smaller BIDs can significantly improve a commercial district's prospects by simply making the area safer and cleaner. Larger BIDs can also concentrate on cultivating economic development.

Downtown districts are realizing measurable success—whether through reduced crime rates or improved property values—in enhancing the future viability of commercial districts in cities of all sizes. For example, the Downtown Denver Partnership is engaged in a focused effort to cultivate a 24-hour downtown environment. In 1992, the partnership created the Center City Housing Support Office (HSO) with the goal of adding 10,000 residents to downtown Denver in ten years, more than double the current number of residents. The HSO's strategy to encourage the development of housing of mixed types and prices is market-driven and project-oriented. The office identified 35 vacant or nearly vacant downtown commercial buildings that it believed could be economically converted to housing. To encourage private investment, it established itself as a "one-stop shop" and acted as a liaison among developers, building owners, lenders, public agencies, and neighborhood organizations. The HSO directly assists developers in obtaining acquisition and construction financing, including finding any public financial assistance for which a project might be eligible. It also provides technical assistance, such as conducting feasibility studies for prospective projects. The results are impressive. Today, 30 of the buildings have been converted to rental or for-sale housing or are undergoing renovation; the rest are in planning.

Project Success Stories

As the following projects illustrate, obsolete buildings can be recycled successfully to accommodate a wide range of market-based uses. In each case, the developer capitalized on several advantages inherent in the existing structure to create a new use.

From Office Tower to Hotel

Three years ago, when Spokane-based developer Goodale & Barbieri (G&B) became interested in entering Seattle's hot hotel market, it scoured the area for a well-located site on which to open a new hotel as quickly as possible. Having already undertaken adaptive use development successfully, G&B was open to considering and eventually pursuing an unconventional alternative—acquiring and converting a vacant 20-story former bank headquarters building in downtown Seattle to a mid-priced 300-room hotel, now called Cavanaugh's Inn.

G&B soon realized that reusing the 1974-vintage office building offered some exceptional advantages. First, the downtown site was perfect for a hotel. It is within walking distance of Seattle's retail, entertainment, cultural, and office districts and is in a business improvement district that provides extra security and cleanup. Second, the prevailing zoning permitted the hotel use and exempted the 240-foot-high office building from an ordinance that now limits height in that part of downtown to 85 feet. Don Barbieri, G&B's president, says that reuse of the existing structure not only enabled G&B to take advantage of the extraordinary height bonus but also shortened the public approval process and construction schedule so much that the company was able to open the hotel a full three years earlier than it would have taken had new construction alternatives been used. A third benefit of recycling the former bank was the existing structure's suitability for the new use. The building is massed with 15 upper floors atop a wider base formed by the first five floors. The smaller floorplates of the upper floors were conducive to an efficient configuration of larger-than-average hotel rooms around the windowed perimeter, with cleaning and storage space in the center. The lower floors were converted to retail, offices, and corporate meeting space.

Funding for the renovation of Cavanaugh's Inn involved a combination of debt financing from a pension fund and the developer's equity. Barbieri says that the total cost of acquiring and converting the bank building was probably comparable to constructing a new hotel. But the value of the location, density bonus, and three-year time savings is beyond measure.

Transforming Commercial Buildings to Housing

Many cities hope that surplus commercial buildings can be successfully transformed into residential uses, and for good reason. New residents bring to a downtown desperately needed activity as well as demand for retail, entertainment, and all types of services; in essence, residents bring community back to the city.

In fact, housing appears to be one of the most feasible reuse opportunities for obsolete buildings. Interest in urban living is increasing even in cities like Houston and Atlanta that traditionally have not had strong center-city residential fundamentals. To be sure, the suburbs still represent the lifestyle of choice for middle-class American families, but a growing percentage of the population does not fit this standard. People in this segment —singles, one-parent families, empty nesters— are attracted to the city for its conveniences, cultural amenities, entertainment, and diversity. This niche market is also the one most likely to appreciate the out-of-the-ordinary quality of rehabilitated older buildings.

Randy Alexander, a Madison, Wisconsin, developer, has transformed over 100 obsolete office and other commercial buildings to successful mixed-income, multifamily properties—in cities such as Racine, Wisconsin; Fort Worth, Texas; and other places—that have "bankers living next to bakers, and fixed-income elderly living next

to professionals." Alexander says that this unorthodox mix has worked well because the units are all distinctive and desirable, regardless of price, and standards for occupancy are uniformly strict.

It takes vision, fortitude, and creative financing to be the first developer to rehabilitate buildings in a transitional neighborhood. Those first few pioneer projects can take advantage of the lowest purchase prices to produce affordable housing alternatives even as their success opens up the area for more development. For Bob Silverman, president of the Winter Group of Companies in Atlanta, his first building conversion took the form of a 65,000-square-foot warehouse in a desolate area near downtown Atlanta populated by old warehouses, abandoned commercial buildings, and vagrants. After having seen local artists use buildings in the neighborhood for art shows, Silverman got the idea that the area could be converted to live/work loft space for artists and cooperative art galleries. After 32 banks refused to finance his first project, Silverman proceeded anyway, using his own equity to convert the warehouse building to an art gallery and offices on the second floor. The project leased up within five months. When the second project—an old candy factory converted into lofts—leased up within three weeks, lenders became more interested. Silverman has gone on to redevelop several more immediately leasable buildings in the area, all with an art component, and the area has now become a burgeoning arts district. Rents for loft apartments in the district area generally have risen to market rates.

Finding a suitable building can be almost as challenging as finding the financing to convert it to housing. After surveying many of lower Manhattan's obsolete office buildings, the Crescent Heights Group selected 25 Broad Street, a turn-of-the-century 21-story office building, to convert to rental apartments. The project, which is in the initial stages of development, is one of the first large-scale building conversions in the area. Project manager Bruce Batkin said that the building's smaller floorplates, one of the qualities that made the structure inefficient for corporate office use, make it a good residential building. However, even with a building depth of less than 75 feet, about 30 percent of the space will be wasted. The building's exterior is well preserved and rich in architectural detail. The interior will be completely gutted and rebuilt, making the process more like new construction. Between the low acquisition price ($10 per square foot) and tax abatements offered by the city for conversion to housing, Crescent will be able to offer larger-than-average apartments at about 20 percent under the price of comparable units in other areas of the city.

Turning Older Buildings into Alternative Office Space

Despite the fact that much of the existing older office space is functionally obsolete for traditional downtown corporate office space, some of it can be renovated for smaller tenants looking for efficient, less expensive office space. Customized, moderately priced office space can also be created from industrial buildings of all types.

Market demand for unconventional office space could increase in the coming years given that much of the nation's economic growth is expected to come from startup and smaller companies, especially in high-tech industries. Such firms often need to be in urban locations to be near major research centers and to attract younger, highly skilled employees, but a lack of lower-cost office and research and development space near downtowns generally forces them to opt for suburban space.

The problems associated with developing office space for small high-tech tenants result less from a shortage of demand than from a shortage of available capital. Construction loans are hard to come by when a project's future tenants are perceived as high credit risks. In addition, such tenants often cannot obtain financing for build-out. Still, some developers have found creative ways to respond to this market. MIT, for example, converted an old automobile assembly plant that it owns in Cambridge, Massachusetts, to multitenant biotech laboratory and office space. MIT financed tenant improvements, which are amortized over the life of each commercial lease, and, as an additional risk premium, acquired stock warrants in the tenant companies, which MIT can exercise if the companies go public.

Albert Friedman's Chicago-based development company, J.A. Friedman & Associates, has found a niche converting older commercial buildings into alternative office space. Over a 20-year period, Friedman has acquired 35 older commercial properties in a once-seedy nine-block area close to Chicago's central business district and converted them to street-level retail and above-ground offices.

Friedman has acquired only "diamonds in the rough," usually dilapidated but structurally sound buildings that have some inherent architectural or historical appeal and, not surprisingly, low purchase prices. Each converted building has its own identity, which the company carefully accentuates in its marketing brochure. Friedman promotes the entire nine-block area, now called Courthouse District, by offering prospective tenants an array of office space, restaurants, and retail amenities. Office tenants in Courthouse District are attracted to the affordability and charm of the neighborhood and prefer the renovated older buildings to more sterile conventional commercial space. ✳

Numerous large office buildings in lower Manhattan are being converted to residential use, including 25 Broad Street, a 21-story structure built in 1896; the building will include 345 rental units when completed.

Urban Parks and Open Space: Enhancing the Urban Realm

Alexander Garvin

Alexander Garvin is a developer, owner, and manager of New York City real estate. Currently a commissioner on the New York City Planning Commission, he also held prominent positions in New York City government from 1970 to 1980. Before entering government, Garvin worked as an architect. He is the author of numerous academic and professional articles and a new book, *The American City: What Works, What Doesn't*, published in 1996 (New York: McGraw-Hill Inc.).

In 1850, the public realm in the United States consisted of unpaved streets, barely landscaped squares, rudimentary marketplaces, and vast territories of wilderness. Everything else was in the hands of property owners whose actions were virtually unregulated. There were as yet no large public parks acquired, developed, and managed specifically as recreational facilities.

Imagine Manhattan if public officials in the mid-19th century had chosen not to spend the money needed to acquire and develop America's first large public park. The New York of today would be without Central Park, an unusually beautiful recreational facility actively used by a quarter of a million people on a typical weekend. Equally important, the city would be collecting far less tax revenue.

Property values in Manhattan doubled during the 15 years after park development began. In the three wards surrounding Central Park, two and one-half miles north of most of the city's real estate activity, values increased nine times.[1] These park-generated tax revenues allowed the city to pay for municipal services that it could not otherwise have afforded and provided the stimulus for city officials to acquire the 26,369 acres of land that now constitute New York City's extraordinary park system.

Now, imagine what life would be like today if cities across the nation had watched New York's rejection of park spending and decided to follow suit. Most cities would have continued to direct their resources to more pressing needs, such as police protection and public education. And the public realm would now consist primarily of streets, roads, and highways—rather than parks.

Fortunately, that didn't happen. Central Park initiated more than a century of government property acquisition and park development in the United States. City, state, and federal agencies now own and operate hundreds of millions of acres. Most of this public realm consists of parkland that was acquired and developed to be a place of refuge from city life, a recreational resource for large numbers of people, a scenic treasure preserved for posterity, or a means of maintaining ecological balance. The very creation of this vast public realm allowed attention to be directed to the many other issues that have come to dominate the public agenda. If the country had not invested in a vast system of public parks, city and suburban residents would still be clamoring for them.

After a century of sustained park development, post–World War II America shifted away from providing the public with additional open space through appropriations; instead, public officials tried to accomplish the same result less expensively, through regulation. One result is that we have become mired in unnecessary political conflicts because community attempts to ensure privacy and security consistently clash with government efforts to guarantee public access to open space.

Such conflicts have deflected public attention away from the increasing demand for recreational facilities brought about by America's population increase of more than 100 million since

World War II. As most cities and suburbs continuously reduce appropriations for park acquisition, development, and maintenance, increasing numbers of people crowd into existing facilities. The result is a growing imbalance between the supply of public open space and the demands of a growing population.

We have forgotten the reasons that Americans in the late 19th and early 20th centuries devoted so much energy and money to creating a vast array of public parks. They understood that judicious public spending on park development stimulates widespread and sustained private investment, alters settlement patterns, encourages social interaction, and reshapes the character of daily life. If we are to supply open space to our growing population, we will have to stop trying to expand the public realm on the cheap through regulation and resume the program of property acquisition and park development that worked so well during the late 19th and early 20th centuries.

Alexander Garvin (1987)

This article examines some of the issues involved in locating and designing public parks that arose during the 19th century—issues that are every bit as significant today. What types of sites are best suited for park development? Where should they be located? What principles should deter-

The Denver Sixteenth Street Mall is 13 blocks long and one block wide. Free bus service, carrying some 100,000 people a day, runs up and down the street and the new light-rail system intersects with Sixteenth Street.

ULI Leadership Counterpoint

Participants in a recent ULI leadership roundtable agreed that using a variety of models within urban park systems was the most reasonable approach to future park development and maintenance to counteract the downsizing of park budgets. "We have to be careful that private parks don't become one more means of further stratifying our society, so people who are less well off cannot access them," cautioned a participant. "That doesn't mean we can't have private space, but we shouldn't have communities that don't have, as part of their community, public space that is maintained and operated for the benefit of the broader public."

Many cities are turning to a model that relies on the intense involvement of the private sector, which can take on some of the traditionally public sector roles, usually through business improvement districts (BIDs). They bring an entrepreneurial cast to the park with self-perpetuating financial and legal mechanisms that help maintain a high operational level of service. But the ULI leadership feared that their success in many cases depends on nearby well-to-do residents and workers and high land costs.

The use of both subcontracting services or redevelopment financing from the private sector is also increasing in urban park programs, including "adopt a park" pro-

grams. In Houston, for example, a city-run golf course was upgraded by corporate sponsors who adopted a hole and paid for an extensive renovation of the deteriorating public golf course.

Additional models suggested by the ULI leadership include

• a quasi-public model being applied to the redevelopment of the Presidio in San Francisco. Run by the National Park Service, this development trust will receive money from the federal government for 12 years, by which time the entire park must be self-sustaining;
• a system of membership cards to handle the problem of suburban residents using parks developed and maintained by the city and not financed by suburban taxes;
• private sector park acquisition and development—but with *state* oversight—when local parks departments lack adequate budgets and management resources;
• bond funds used to acquire and maintain parks, such as in Dade County, Los Angeles, and Gwinnett County (Georgia);
• combined schools and parks (as in Kansas City and Chicago) to provide steadier use as well as built-in security and maintenance. However, a new set of security issues must be dealt with in this situation; and

• municipal requirements that developers contribute 1 percent for parks instead of 1 percent for public art. Much of the public art that has been provided generates little activity and may not be well maintained.

The participants agreed that in every type of development—master-planned communities, apartment and condominium developments, retail developments, and office developments—parks are the most important amenity today, more so than active amenities. "One can easily measure the value of the park by the value of the surrounding real estate," said one participant. "Even though parks are complicated sociological situations, if they're managed properly they much enhance rents and the values surrounding property." Participants agreed that commercial property owners today would in many cases gladly take over the maintenance of a nearby park and tax themselves to maintain it so that it becomes a plus to the neighborhood—not a negative. "Seldom do people speak against parks," noted one participant. "They're like motherhood."

This counterpoint is a summary of a roundtable discussion at the ULI Midwinter Leadership Meeting in Boca Raton, Florida, February 1997.

Originally proposed as "Greensward" by its designers, Central Park in Manhattan today accommodates a wonderful variety of landscapes and built features that are cherished by visitors.

Alexander Garvin (1994)

mine their design? How should they be financed? Who should own and manage them?

The article also examines the role of other forms of publicly owned open space, including squares, marketplaces, and streets. Finally, it reviews some recent approaches to park design, financing, and management that provide promising models for future action.

19th-Century Park Development and Design

Writing in 1870, landscape architect Frederick Law Olmsted described Prospect Park in Brooklyn and Central Park in Manhattan as "the only places" in those cities where "vast numbers of persons [are] brought closely together, poor and rich, young and old . . . each individual adding by his mere presence to the pleasure of all others."[2] These parks had been open to the public for less than a decade when Olmsted made these statements, yet merely the decision to acquire land for them had already spurred development of countless parks in other cities.

Today, most city governments operate and maintain a large inventory of such mixing valves for their increasingly diverse populations. The New York City Department of Parks and Recreation manages 18 miles of beaches; 46 swimming pools; 16 golf courses; six skating rinks; and 1,570 parks, playgrounds, and public spaces. The Minneapolis Park and Recreation Board, serving a population less than 5 percent of New York City's, has a system of 6,380 acres containing 170 park properties, including 42 recreation centers, 61 supervised

playgrounds, 21 beaches, and 22 major still-water lakes.

Park systems like these do not just happen. They are the product of myriad decisions taken over decades by hundreds of public officials. Those decisions include where parks should be located; for whom they should be provided; how they should be designed; how to pay for them; who should be responsible for management and maintenance; and how to maximize desirable spillover benefits for surrounding communities.

From the beginning, there was controversy over such decisions. Public officials looked for ways to purchase properties at low prices. Land that was not easy to develop, because of steep slopes, drainage difficulties, or some other problem, was usually the least expensive to acquire, and was consequently appealing to budget-conscious public officials. Often these sites were no more appropriate for park development than for private construction, but they were acquired anyway.

The first parks proposed by George Kessler for Kansas City in 1893 were located on steep slopes that were unattractive for real estate development. Even so, the Board of Park Commissioners faced opposition from citizens concerned about the loss of real estate tax revenues. Consequently, in 1899 the board eliminated from these sites the most easily developable land. Only when the remaining relatively poor sites proved to be popular did the commissioners begin acquiring larger, more accessible properties more suitable for park development.

The romantic landscapes that Olmsted created on the sites of Brooklyn's Prospect Park and Manhattan's Central Park became models for most 19th-century parks. In St. Louis, landscape gardener Maximillian G. Kern copied the Olmstedian rolling meadows and curving pedestrian paths in 1876, when he transformed 1,372 acres on the outskirts of St. Louis into Forest Park.[3] Like so many of Olmsted's followers, however, he believed that a sylvan setting was all that was needed. Consequently, he paid scant attention to the needs of the large numbers of people who used the park. By 1915, St. Louis had begun to alter this inadequate design because, as its department of parks explained, "The primary purpose of the park system has become the raising of men and women rather than grass or trees." None of Olmsted's work required alteration because he always designed for active use by large numbers of people.

These 19th-century examples demonstrate that acquiring property and labeling it parkland is not enough to create facilities in which "vast numbers of persons [are] brought closely together." The property must be located in places easily accessible to vast numbers of people, and its topography must provide them with suitable gathering places. The arrangement of grass and bushes and trees must be capable of withstanding heavy pedestrian traffic. As Olmsted explained when designing the Boston park system, "A site for a park to stand by itself and be little used except by those living near it should be a very different one from that for a park designed for more general use, and especially for a park which is to stand in a series."[4]

Current Park Development Strategies

By the second half of the 20th century, most cities had invested in major park systems. Yet their residents were moving to the suburbs, where they believed there were better opportunities for recreation. In fact, the very suburbs to which city dwellers moved were seriously lacking public parkland. It was too late to create major public parks in these areas because the best sites had already been developed as residential subdivisions. While suburban areas had growing populations, most residents were unwilling to vote for the increased taxes needed to pay for public parks.

City residents were as unwilling to pay for parkland as their suburban counterparts. With the exception of Minneapolis, Boulder, and a small number of other cities, spending on parks has been steadily cut. In New York City, for example, during the 1940s and 1950s, when Robert Moses was parks commissioner, parks accounted for approximately 1.5 percent of the annual operating budget. By the 1990s, this figure had dropped to less than half a percent. In suburban areas, where recreational facilities consist of swimming pools, gyms, public golf courses, and school ballfields, spending levels are often still lower.

After World War II, government action to increase the availability of public open space shifted away from new park development to other strategies. Perhaps this was because most cities (though few suburbs) already had impressive parks, or because of the mounting cost of operating extensive park systems, or because there were other, more important demands for public expenditures. The two most popular strategies used in recent years have been to make available for recreational purposes other government-owned property (especially land used by motor vehicles) and to require property owners to make increasing amounts of their land available for public use. Both approaches are fraught with controversy. The first increases competition among different groups who believe they are entitled to use publicly owned property. The other sharpens antagonism between private property owners and the civic and government organizations seeking to increase the public realm.

Retrofitting Streets as Pedestrian Open Space

It is misleading to think of parkland as the only form of open space available to the public. Large numbers of people come together in other places that are publicly owned but that have not been acquired strictly for recreational purposes—streets, squares, and marketplaces. It is important to understand how such spaces work and to make them an integral part of a community's total open-space strategy.

Retail streets, squares, and marketplaces, like parks, act as mixing valves for large numbers of people. Long before they began acquiring land specifically for public recreation, governments provided town greens, public commons, and squares. As a result, city residents became accustomed to strolling and gathering in places such as the Boston Common, the New Haven Green, and New Orleans's Plâce d'Armes (now Jackson Square).

Just as public squares are often overlooked as recreation sites, so are marketplaces. For decades, Seattle's Pike Place Market and Los Angeles's Farmers' Market have played much more important roles as tourist destinations than as local shopping facilities. More than 200 crafts vendors come together in Portland, Oregon, for Saturday Market, which continues throughout the weekend and attracts more than 10,000 people from all over the metropolitan area.

Almost half a century has passed since architect Victor Gruen proposed an obvious solution to the lack of public squares and pedestrian-oriented marketplaces in central cities: banish motor vehicles from selected streets and retrofit them as public open spaces. Such "pedestrianized" streets can then be designed and managed in a manner that allows downtown merchants to compete with those in shopping centers.

Gruen based his proposal on Rotterdam's Lijnbaan, a 3,000-foot-long retail street that replaced the tangle of arteries destroyed by aerial bombing early in World War II. The Lijnbaan, which opened in 1953, looked more like a shopping center than a city street. Gruen recognized immediately that similar shopping precincts could be created in cities across the United States. He proposed to do so by removing the roadbed; installing appropriate paving; providing new lighting and street furniture; requiring consistent signage; and adding trees, flowers, and other landscape elements.

In 1958, Kalamazoo, Michigan, became the first American city to adopt Gruen's ideas. Within a few years, similar projects were underway in Miami, Knoxville, Fresno, Providence, Honolulu, and countless other cities. In some cities, like Providence, the creation of a pedestrian mall was not enough to keep shoppers downtown. But whether or not these retrofitted arterials were successful in attracting and retaining retail shoppers, they did substantially increase the amount of open space available to the public.

Pedestrianization is an attractive approach to increasing public open space because it does not cost governments much money. Nothing has to be spent on land acquisition. Construction, management, and maintenance can be charged to surrounding property owners. There is no cheaper way to provide citizens with additional public open space. Local governments are also able to transfer to the private sector a large portion of the cost of street maintenance. Properties within Minneapolis's Nicollet Mall special assessment district, for example, pay 90 percent of the maintenance costs.

Nicollet Mall proved successful for several reasons: it takes less than ten minutes to walk from one end to the other; virtually all the city's office, retail, hotel, and convention facilities are within a block or two of the mall; and the mall was planned in conjunction with the city's skywalks and parking garages. A similarly critical mass of facilities is clustered along Denver's Sixteenth Street Mall. In this case, the city's main office, retail, hotel, and convention facilities are combined with the state capitol, a performing arts center, a university, and two suburban bus terminals.

In many other cities, however, pedestrian malls have been dismal failures. They failed because public officials erroneously thought that success was merely a matter of removing motor vehicles, repaving, and adding glitzy street furniture—just as they had earlier erroneously thought that successful parks were merely a matter of acquiring property and planting grass and trees.

Transforming Highways into Parks

Reclaiming highways, another attractive way to increase public open space, also requires virtually no expenditures on acquisition and no lengthy land assembly process. Freeway Park in Seattle is the most imaginative example of this strategy. When Interstate 5 opened in 1965, it cut downtown Seattle in half, creating an unwanted division between the central business district and nearby commercial and institutional activity. More important, the interstate had a blighting effect along both edges of the highway. Public officials decided to knit together the two sections of the city by building a park on top of the highway. When Lawrence Halprin & Associates completed this five-acre facility in 1976, the park increased the attractiveness of sites for office buildings and retail stores in the business district to the west of the freeway and for residences and institutions to the east. Indeed, the project was so successful that in 1984 an additional two-acre section of the freeway was covered to extend the park.

Development costs for highway transformation can often be charged to federal and state governments. In Portland, Oregon, a multilane freeway encircling the business district rendered superfluous Portland's main highway bypass, six-lane Harbor Drive, which ran along the Willamette River. The removal of Harbor Drive in 1974 provided a unique opportunity to reclaim 2.75 miles of prime waterfront land as public open space—making it possible to create Tom McCall Park without causing traffic problems or relocating residents or businesses.

Another such transformation occurred in Boston, where the city cleared a wide swath of land running from the Back Bay and South End to Jamaica Plain and Roxbury for a highway that was never constructed. The 4.7-mile route became Southwest Corridor Park, created on a platform over the relocated Orange subway line. The city is now in the process of burying the Central Artery, the elevated highway separating downtown Boston from its North End waterfront, and creating a 20-acre linear park by platforming over the buried highway.

When the 1989 Loma Prieta earthquake rendered the Embarcadero Freeway unusable, San Francisco replaced it with an at-grade boulevard that includes a palm-lined tramway and a 25-foot-wide pedestrian promenade. This narrow linear park is punctuated by artwork and provides space for jogging, bicycling, and other forms of recreation.

New York City is creating a similar linear park along Route 9A, which runs at grade along the Hudson River in Lower Manhattan. If all goes as planned, the new Hudson River Park will include a five-mile waterfront esplanade connecting 13 renovated public recreation piers, ballfields, playgrounds, boating facilities, and the Chelsea Piers (a privately financed and developed sports and entertainment complex). Hudson River Park will be separated from the rest of Manhattan by six to eight lanes of vehicular traffic.

The nearly $330 million capital cost of this new linear park will come primarily from city, state, and federal funds. That is the park's only similarity to a conventional public park that is managed and maintained by a city parks department. The Hudson River Park is managed by the Hudson River Park Conservancy, a nonprofit subsidiary of New York State's Empire Development Corporation.[5] Properties such as the Chelsea Piers, along the right-of-way of Route 9A, will generate lease and concession revenues to cover the park's operating expenses.

Using Parking Garage Revenues to Pay for Parks

Another way to minimize the cost of acquiring, developing, and maintaining public open space is to use it simultaneously for automobiles and people. San Francisco pioneered this strategy in 1940, when it opened a 1,700-car public parking garage under Union Square, a traditional, landscaped, 2.6-acre park that had been donated to the city in 1850. Los Angeles did the same from 1950 to 1951 when it dug up Pershing Square, its five-acre downtown park, to provide 2,150 underground parking spaces.

While garage revenues defrayed the cost of maintaining Union and Pershing squares, these projects did not add one square inch of public open space to either city. Pittsburgh was the first city to use parking demand to provide an income stream that would cover debt service on the capital borrowed to pay the cost of developing and maintaining a new park. In 1948, Pittsburgh's Public Parking Authority proposed building a six-story garage on the 1.37-acre site that is now Mellon Square. The following year, the Mellon family offered to pay for the construction of a park on this site. In exchange, the city agreed to build the garage underneath the park. Now, Mellon Square is a park that occupies a 230-foot-by-260-foot block, right in the middle of downtown Pittsburgh.

A growing number of cities now provide parking under public parks, including Grant Park (Chicago), the Boston Common, and Market Square (Alexandria, Virginia). Some, such as Mellon Square in Pittsburgh and Post Office Square in Boston, include retail and other uses that enhance daily life in the surrounding city. Post Office Square, for example, includes a café/restaurant, creating consumer traffic that integrates the park into the daily life of downtown Boston. The planners of Post Office Square recognized that small, center-city parks had to be

The five-mile-long Southwest Corridor Park in Boston was part of a $780 million transit project that combined an existing commuter railroad, a new subway line, and vacant and underused property.

Alexander Garvin (1994)

Alexander Garvin (1996)

made a part of the complex mix of activities that take place in downtown locations and could not simply be refuges from the city's busy streets.

Reclaiming Waterways as Public Open Space

Perhaps the most appealing way to recapture public open space is to make waterfronts accessible and attractive. Many cities think of their waterfronts in the limited way that Olmsted warned against. Los Angeles is the perfect example. In 1914, when the Los Angeles River overflowed, causing $10 million in damage, engineers recommended channelization. Flooding caused 40 deaths in 1934 and 59 in 1938. The city's solution was, in 1939, to relegate 46 miles of the Los Angeles River's 58-mile route through the city to concrete culverts fenced off from the public. Los Angeles no longer experiences serious flooding, but by investing in a single-function capital improvement, the city missed its opportunity to create a rich and varied 58-mile public park that would also have solved an environmental problem.

The citizens of San Antonio were much wiser. From the early 1920s until the mid-1930s, they kept public officials from implementing an engineering solution to San Antonio's flooding problems. When the city government proposed relegating the horseshoe-shaped, downtown section of the San Antonio River to a concrete conduit and creating a new downtown street by paving over it, citizens demanded that the riverfront be transformed into a public park. Money for this project did not become available until 1939, when the Works Progress Administration (WPA) agreed to provide $300,000 if the city put up

$75,000. The city raised the needed matching funds by issuing bonds.

Paseo del Rio, as this new park was called, opened in 1941. The city solved the flooding problems by dredging a bypass channel across the open end of the horseshoe and installing locks at either end. Whenever necessary, these locks are closed so that floodwaters can be channeled away from the riverfront park.

"Public" Open Space on "Private" Property

The least expensive way to provide public open space in developed areas is to have property owners create, manage, and maintain it. Although the fourteenth amendment to the Constitution explicitly forbids states (and therefore local governments) from taking property for public use without compensation, it does not preclude local governments from encouraging owners to provide access to their property for public use. Consequently, local governments have enacted a variety of incentives to induce property owners to expand the public realm.

New York City adopted the incentive approach in 1961, when it added to its zoning resolution an as-of-right incentive for property owners who provided publicly accessible open areas. In certain high-density residential or commercial zones, developers were permitted additional floor area in exchange for any sidewalk or plaza space added to the public realm.

Although the incentive arrangement included minimum design standards, these standards were not always sufficient to encourage the use and enjoyment of the new public spaces. Consequently, the city planning commission introduced a series of zoning changes that refined the design standards, established safety and maintenance requirements, allowed nighttime closing, and increased the areas in which street-wall requirements precluded plaza development.

In 1996, after 35 years of experience, much of it unsatisfactory, the planning commission decided to eliminate outmoded requirements and upgraded others. It also consolidated the confusing array of piecemeal provisions into a zoning text amendment that simplified, reorganized, and improved regulations covering plazas, arcades, covered pedestrian spaces, and public gallerias.

In the suburbs, there are currently two approaches to preserving open space, involving either incentives or regulations. The first allows developers to build more than the ordinarily allowable number of houses, if the houses are arranged in a manner that protects attractive landscape features and provides common open space. This alternative to yard and setback requirements, called planned unit development (PUD), began to be added to zoning ordinances and subdivision regulations during the 1960s. The second approach is to require that site plans comply with state and local environmental legislation. This approach became prevalent during the 1970s and 1980s, as state after state enacted such legislation. On the other hand, more recent master-planned communities, such as Rancho Santa Margarita and Kentlands, include substantial areas for active recreation by large numbers of people.

Unlike large-scale, master-planned communities, the PUD approach is based on simple economics. Small subdivisions usually cannot afford to provide the amenities that are routinely supplied in large-scale, master-planned communities. The PUD approach, however, provides developers of smaller subdivisions with an economic incentive. In exchange for an improved site plan and community amenities, the project is permitted to include a greater number of dwellings than would be permitted by conventional zoning. Developers readily adopt this alternative to standardized subdivisions when the profit from selling the additional dwellings exceeds the additional cost of complying with PUD requirements. As a result, PUDs are often tailored to the natural features of their sites and provide amenities that are not available in a conventional subdivision.

Despite improved site plans and attractive open spaces that can be enjoyed by their occupants,

PUDs have provided little open space that is clearly earmarked for the general public. Unlike the city zoning bonus that requires public access to plaza space, the suburban PUD bonus has no such requirement. Most people are unaware of the open space because it is usually located behind private homes. Moreover, residents concerned with privacy and security routinely discourage strangers from intruding into their carefully planned environment. As a result, by the 1990s, much of the open space provided by PUD developers was used primarily by PUD residents and their guests, and, in the case of gated communities, was unavailable to the public.

State and local environmental protection statutes have had a similarly limited effect on suburban open space development. Faced with litigation or the threat of litigation, most developers eventually negotiate site plans that are acceptable to environmentalists: they agree not to develop wetlands, steep slopes, sensitive habitats, and other problem areas, which they then generously designate as "open space." As a result, many new master-planned communities include vast amounts of open space that is specifically designed to be difficult to use by community residents.

Like the cheap land that was purchased for city parks during the 19th century, much of this "open space" is no more attractive for active public recreation than for construction. But unlike those early parks, many of these environmentally sensitive areas are closed to the public. Thus, residents of newly developing suburban areas whose environments have been "protected" have even less usable public open space than they left behind in the city.

New Directions

Many of the case studies in ULI's forthcoming book *Urban Parks and Open Space* illustrate the continuing effort to adapt and reuse underused and abandoned city land for recreational purposes. There still are plenty of city streets and railroad rights-of-way that can be reclaimed as vehicle-free, public open space, just as there are miles of largely vacant waterfront that can become usable parkland. And these are not the only opportunities. Plenty of land once used for industrial manufacturing sits vacant because the costs of cleaning it up and retrofitting it for public use are high, or because obsolete zoning prohibits reuse for nonindustrial purposes.

Similar opportunities exist in suburban areas, which harbor the same underused streets and railroad rights-of-way, abandoned waterfronts, and empty manufacturing plants found in cities. The suburbs also have opportunities that cannot be found in cities. Air-conditioned shopping malls and "big-box" retailers have forced many strip malls and open-air shopping centers out of business. Such areas can be purchased at relatively low prices and redesigned as public parks.

The key to exploiting these opportunities, however, is not the creation of ever-more-inventive land use regulations. So far, regulation has succeeded primarily in producing a large number of unsatisfactory public spaces, taking huge amounts of land out of public use, and triggering a property rights backlash that may succeed in reversing important efforts to improve the environment. It is time to abandon our efforts to make property owners supply public open space and to redirect our energies to persuading the electorate to invest in public parks.

The main obstacle is money. Public officials are no more willing to increase spending on park development today than they were a century ago. But the opposing argument, given by the Minneapolis Board of Trade in 1883, is as valid today as it was then: parkland, "when secured and located as [it] can now be at comparatively small expense, will in the near future add many millions to the real estate value of [the] city."[6]

The wisdom of this advice is illustrated by Pioneer Courthouse Square in Portland, Oregon. The city purchased the site for $3 million in 1979, just before property values escalated, and invested an additional $4.3 million in the development of the square. When Pioneer Courthouse Square opened in 1984 at the intersection of Portland's pedestrianized streets and light-rail transit system, it became the most convenient spot in downtown Portland. Nordstrom built a new store opposite the square. The Rouse Company converted the nearby Olds & King Department Store into the Galleria, a 75-foot-high shopping atrium. Saks Fifth Avenue and Pioneer Place (a multistory shopping arcade) opened a block away. There are few better examples of public open space acquired "at comparatively small expense" that "in the near future add [so] many millions to the real estate value of [the] city."

Most public officials are not courageous enough to spend $7.3 million to transform less than an acre of prime real estate into public open space. There are too many other competing public purposes (preventing crime, educating children, moving traffic, etc.) that have larger constituen-

cies. Public officials would, however, support creation of additional public open space if they did not have to appropriate the money. Fortunately, Minneapolis, Boulder, Denver, and New York City have devised a mechanism that allows this to happen: *the dedicated tax.*

From its inception in 1883, the Minneapolis Park and Recreation Board has been allocated a portion of the city's real estate tax revenue. This guaranteed revenue stream has allowed the park board to plan for land acquisition, park development, and ongoing maintenance without worrying about competition with other more powerful city agencies or more popular public objectives.

Boulder allocates a portion of its sales tax to acquire and develop public parks. Its citizens do so because they wish to preserve the foothills of the Rocky Mountains as public land, to create a greenbelt encircling the city and protecting it from suburban sprawl, to maintain the wide range of ecosystems that characterize the area, and to provide in-town recreational facilities. In 1967, the city dedicated to park purposes a sales tax of $.004 per dollar. During the next 18 years, the city added 12,000 acres to its park system. The impact of these additions to public open space was that by 1977, the price of a house was higher by $4.20 for every foot that the house was nearer to the greenbelt.[7] The city was sufficiently impressed that in 1989 it voted to raise this dedicated tax to $.0073 per dollar. Consequently, Boulder now contains more than 40,000 acres of public open space—quite impressive for a city that has not yet reached a population of 100,000.

More recently, property owners have been willing to pay additional real estate taxes to support business improvement districts (BIDs). Initially, BIDs were used as an equitable way to pay for the cost of pedestrianizing shopping streets, maintaining and patrolling the newly created public open spaces, and financing promotional activities that allowed city merchants to compete with suburban shopping centers.

The Downtown Denver Partnership, for example, operates the Sixteenth Street Mall Management District. Its work is financed by assessments on 865 property owners within the 120-block district surrounding this 13-block-long public open space. The money is spent on maintaining trees, flowers, and other plantings; sweeping pavements, removing litter, and emptying trash receptacles; providing security services; programming outdoor entertainment; and all the other services that make the Sixteenth Street

Boulder's dedicated sales tax makes it possible for the city to acquire and maintain more than 40,000 acres of park properties.

Alexander Garvin (1993)

Mall one of the most successful public spaces in the country.

Manhattan's Bryant Park BID is financed in a similar way. However, in 1996, real estate taxes provided less than half of its $1.9 million operating budget. The city department of parks continues to pay the $250,000 it paid before transferring management to the Bryant Park Restoration Corporation. The rest comes from concession revenues, sales, grants, and park rentals.

The success of Denver's Sixteenth Street BID and Manhattan's Bryant Park BID is not just a matter of creating a dedicated income stream to pay for intelligently designed and well-maintained public open space. In both instances, the BID also pays for the type of aggressive, entrepreneurial management that would be impossible within standard government bureaucracies.

Denver's Sixteenth Street Mall and Manhattan's Bryant Park are models for future open space development. They demonstrate the effectiveness of a dedicated tax, combined with entrepreneurial management that is directly accountable to nearby property owners and, in a more general way, to the broader public. Unfortunately, this model is usable only in situations where surrounding building occupants are willing and able to pay for facilities and services that they would not otherwise have available. Areas with substantial numbers of low-income residents or marginal businesses are unable to generate the necessary money—which is all the more reason for citywide expenditures for public parks.

As an increasing number of communities adopt these new entrepreneurial approaches, we will be in a position to create substantial amounts of new, usable public space in both cities and suburbs. If we do so, we will be able to pick up where the park advocates of the early 20th century left off, discard the more recent attempts to create public open space on the cheap, and resume the effort to provide every American with the parks that Olmsted advocated more than a century ago— places where "vast numbers of persons [are] brought closely together, poor and rich, young and old . . . each individual adding by his mere presence to the pleasure of all others." ✳

Notes

1. Tom Fox, *Urban Open Space—An Investment That Pays* (New York: The Neighborhood Open Space Coalition, 1990), p. 11.

2. Frederick Law Olmsted, "Public Parks and the Enlargement of Towns" (Paper prepared for the American Social Science Association at the Lowell Institute, February 25, 1870). Reprinted in *Civilizing American Cities*, S. B. Sutton, ed. (Cambridge, Mass.: MIT Press, 1971), p. 75.

3. Forest Park was later reduced to 1,293 acres.

4. Frederick Law Olmsted, Seventh Annual Report of the Board of Commissioners of the Department of Parks for the City of Boston for the Year 1881.

5. Formerly the New York State Urban Development Corporation (UDC).

6. Resolution of the Minneapolis Board of Trade, 29 January 1883, quoted by Theodore Wirth in *Minneapolis Park System 1883–1944* (Minneapolis: Minneapolis Board of Park Commissioners, 1945), p. 19.

7. Mark R. Correll, Jane Lillydahl, and Larry D. Singell, "The Effects of Greenbelts on Residential Property Values," *Land Economics* 54 (1978), pp. 205–217.

The Pros and Cons of the Current Pattern of Growth And Development in Metropolitan Areas

J. Thomas Black

J. Thomas Black is an urban development economist and a fellow of the Lincoln Institute of Land Policy. He is a former resident fellow of ULI specializing in urban development economics and finance, and prior to that served as staff vice president for research, education, and publications.

For the past 120 years or so, urban growth has involved a predominantly outward expansion of development (houses, roads, stores, manufacturing facilities, and office buildings) from what originally were highly compact urban centers closely tied to transportation facilities such as railroads, hubs, or ports. As a result, most of us live and work today in low-density, multicentered metropolitan complexes that developed around original urban centers.

Over the last decade, this prevailing low-density, loosely knit, multicentered pattern of development has been subjected to increasing criticism. In California, a coalition including the Bank of America, the California Resources Agency (a state government conservation agency), the Greenbelt Alliance (a Bay Area citizen conservation and planning organization), and the Low-Income Housing Fund issued a "call for California to move beyond sprawl and rethink the way we grow in the future." Perhaps because a major sponsor was one of the country's largest banks, the coalition's report, entitled "Beyond Sprawl: A New Pattern of Growth to Fit the New California," has generated considerable attention over the past year or two.

The concerns of various critics can be grouped into three major categories that are related but differ markedly in how they should be addressed from a public policy perspective. The categories center around

• concerns about the overall optimization efficiency of development patterns at the metropolitan level (e.g., a bias in infrastructure financing

toward new construction will result in an inefficient system overall);

• concerns about the equity and distributional effects of outlying development on poorer residents left behind in older, core area jurisdictions; and

• concerns about quality and efficiency of development at the neighborhood level.

This paper focuses primarily on the first category, which will be referred to as the metropolitan form issue. Given today's renewed interest in the general question of whether the continued extension of the low-density, multicentered urban complex is desirable or undesirable, it seems timely to review the arguments and evidence and to isolate the key issues underlying the debate.

Characterizing Prevailing Metropolitan Development Patterns

Despite substantial differences regarding what is desirable and undesirable about current metropolitan development patterns, there does seem to be general agreement on what the patterns are. Most serious students of the subject also acknowledge that the patterns vary somewhat from place to place, although some characteristics apply generally, if not to all cases.

Concentration of the U.S. Population in Limited Urban Areas

Based on the Bureau of the Census definition, the United States accounted for 271 metropolitan areas in 1994—253 Metropolitan Statistical Areas (MSAs) and 18 Consolidated Metropolitan Statistical Areas (CMSAs). Of the 265 million people in the United States, about 80 percent—212 million—live in metropolitan areas. The land area within these defined metropolitan areas includes about 16 percent of the total U.S. land. However, not all of the land in these metropolitan areas is developed, and much of it is in open space or farmland. Even after decades of sprawl, the population within metropolitan areas remains highly concentrated. Again, using Bureau of the Census definitions, urban areas in 1990 (urbanized areas plus urban places) represented only 12 percent of the total land area inside metropolitan areas, yet metropolises housed 86 percent of the total metropolitan population.[1] To put it another way, 70 percent of the total population of the United States is concentrated on less than 2 percent of the total U.S. land area within the urban portions of metropolitan areas. From this perspective, it would appear that the overall population of the United States is heavily concentrated relative to the total land expanse of the United States.

The population is also much more heavily concentrated today than it was 50 to 100 years ago, when a less urbanized pattern prevailed. Since 1980, the population of metropolitan areas, as defined in 1995, has grown at about three times that of nonmetropolitan areas (17.2 percent versus 6.6 percent), resulting in an even further relative concentration of the U.S. population in metropolitan areas. But, geographically speaking, the population is even more heavily concentrated. Within the 271 metropolitan areas, the 40 areas with the largest population (just 15 percent of the 271) have 138.7 million people, or 67 percent of the 208 million metropolitan population and over half (53 percent) of the total U.S. population.

Dispersed Multicentered Commercial and Industrial Activity

Cities' commercial and industrial functions have been decentralizing for many decades. Industrial activity began decentralization with the advent of the railroads, which offered more attractive intercity shipping options. By the first part of the 20th century, most of the early industrial cities experienced the development of extended industrial corridors radiating five to ten miles from the core. This, of course, spurred residential development adjacent to the extended industrial areas and, in turn, small commercial-retail strips that served residents and workers. The introduction of extensive streetcar systems in the late 19th century resulted in even farther outward extension of industrial, residential, and

ULI Leadership Counterpoint

The combination of basic real estate economics and strong quality-of-life preferences tends to favor lower-density, multi-centered urbanization patterns rather than high-density, monocentric patterns, according to ULI leadership roundtable participants. Participants recognized that the widespread preference for relatively dispersed, low-density development tends to deemphasize some of the negative side effects of this form of development, particularly the economic decline of older core areas. But, as one member put it, the overriding question is whether, all things considered, life in U.S. metropolitan areas is better than that in countries where urban development is constrained to much more limited areas. For most roundtable participants, the answer was a resounding "yes."

Discussion also touched on the need for and desirability of more flexibility in land use and zoning policy and regulations to permit more latitude in meeting market demand, particularly for alternative housing types and subdivision design. Further, some felt that there was room for im-

provement in the approach to infrastructure financing to ensure both equitable and efficient infrastructure investment.

On the issue of whether metropolitan growth itself was going to be an issue given the shift to knowledge-based work and technological advances in communication and information processing, all participants seemed to think that, on net for both people and businesses, metropolitan areas would retain the advantage over nonmetropolitan areas for the foreseeable future. Thus, the question of accommodating further growth within existing metropolitan areas will be an issue that must be addressed.

The issue of greatest concern was how to address the decline of older core areas. The discussants strongly agreed that, in most areas, efforts to establish significant growth boundary limits around existing urbanized areas would not be effective by themselves in redirecting growth back into depopulated urban cores. Rather, to reuse and revitalize these areas, steps must be taken first to address the social

problems of the low-income population and then to make the areas attractive locations for a significant portion of households and businesses, which means addressing the problems of crime, high taxes, educational deficiencies, physical blight, and often high redevelopment costs.

Most of the participants felt that our society must address these problems or face unacceptable costs over the long term. While the participants did not reach consensus on the solution to the problems of core areas, they evidenced some optimism about the future based on the substantial CBD office base in most areas, expanding urban entertainment activities, the successful development of market-rate housing in many areas, the waterfront locations in most core areas, and the established institutional base.

This counterpoint is a summary of a roundtable discussion at the ULI Midwinter Leadership Meeting in Boca Raton, Florida, February 1997.

commercial development to form a star-shaped pattern in most urban areas. The introduction of the automobile in the early 20th century led to infilling of the areas between the rail corridors and, of course, facilitated the pursuit of cheaper land and more open environments still farther out from predominantly developed areas.

In the last three decades, the business management, finance, and professional service functions, which had remained concentrated in the core CBD up to the 1970s, have decentralized at a rapid rate, leading to the creation of many multiuse suburban business districts with office, retail, and hotel functions, but at much lower densities than in traditional CBDs. In several cases, such as the Tysons Corner area of Fairfax County, Virginia, or South Coast Plaza in Costa Mesa, California, the total office employment in major suburban nodes is greater than that in most traditional downtowns. Furthermore, as these areas have grown, they have spawned the development and expansion of nearby educational and cultural institutions, such as George Mason University and the University of California–Irvine in Orange County.

In short, as several authors have noted, the former suburbs have generally changed from predominantly residential enclaves dependent on the central city for jobs and cultural activity to more independent, cosmopolitan places with a full range of economic activity and a fairly diversified residential base. These new urban places tend to overlap multiple local jurisdictions and involve a complex interacting web of office, industrial, retail, and residential areas.

Today, a major share of commercial and industrial activity is dispersed around the edges of urban areas, with significant concentrations in what have been dubbed "edge cities," while the majority of workers reside outside the traditional central city. Moreover, over the last two decades, approximately two-thirds of all net new metropolitan-based jobs have been created in urban centers outside the central city.

Low Urban Densities
Urban densities in the United States generally tend to be relatively low compared to those in other countries. In 1990, the urbanized portions of metropolitan areas had an average gross population density of 2,593 people per square mile (ppsm), or the equivalent net residential density of three housing units to the acre; central places had an average density of 3,320 ppsm while fringe areas had an average density of 2,130 ppsm.

Among the 25 largest urbanized areas, overall densities ranged from a high of 5,409 ppsm in the New York City urban area (with the poster child of sprawl—Los Angeles—running a close second at 5,140) to a low of 1,673 ppsm in the Kansas City area and 1,898 ppsm in the Atlanta area.

Generally, even the large central cities of the United States are developed at relatively low densities compared to European and other international cities. In 1992, the 77 central cities with populations over 200,000 had, on average, 4,900 people per square mile—a population density equivalent to a gross housing density of three units per acre.[2] When New York City, Newark, Boston, Philadelphia, San Francisco, and Chicago are excluded from the group, the average gross density drops to 4,000 people per square mile, or the equivalent of about 2.5 housing units per gross acre. And these are the mostly built-out cities, not the suburbs. By adding the urbanized portion of the suburbs at average densities closer to 2,100 people per square mile, the overall density for the total urbanized area in the United States averages about 2,600 people per square mile, or about 1.5 housing units per gross acre.

Further, general population growth trends over the past 20 years and in the last few years have tended to reduce population densities in the older, higher-density core areas and to extend the population at the fringe at density levels slightly higher than previous levels. The net effect is that overall density levels for the 25 largest urbanized areas have remained at roughly the same level (3,434 ppsm) while overall densities dropped by 3 percent—from 2,675 ppsm to 2,593 ppsm—for all urbanized areas. Several urbanized areas have experienced a significant increase in population density from 1980 to 1990. For example, Phoenix added about 600,000 people in its urbanized area while adding only 100 square miles to produce a 23 percent increase in population density. San Diego grew by 644,000 people but added only 79 square miles for a 22 percent density increase.

With a strong and widespread trend toward dispersed, multinodal metropolitan development now in its 12th decade and the vast majority of urban America now living in single-family homes or garden apartments in extended postsuburban communities, one obvious conclusion might be that the social and economic forces leading to this form of settlement are particularly strong and reflect the lifestyle and housing preferences of a substantial share of the population. Indeed, if this pattern resulted from inefficient development decisions over several decades, it would be rea-

The prevailing low-density multicentered pattern of development in metropolitan areas has, over the last decade, been subjected to increasing criticism from many quarters. Pictured is the Teleport on Staten Island in New York City, a state-of-the-art business park surrounded by residential areas.

sonable to expect the inefficiencies to show up in above-normal public service costs, above-normal area costs of living, and below-normal economic and population growth rates. In fact, the results appear to be the opposite, as is borne out in the following discussion.

The Pros and Cons of Current Development Patterns

Before getting too far into a discussion of the costs and benefits of alternative development patterns, it should be noted that there is no way to arrive at objectively determined net costs or benefits because there are many real or potential costs and benefits that are not factored into our market pricing systems. In an open economy, where business activity and households can readily move or take business elsewhere, it is difficult to determine how an action will affect the overall system, much less estimate the dollar value of the impact. Moreover, the interactions among many of the factors are complex and, given our current knowledge, impossible to model even in rough quantitative terms. Thus, we are left with only informed judgments, inference from available indicators, and political calculus to make policy decisions while continuing to improve the

knowledge base for making policy decisions regarding metropolitan land use and development. Without even attempting to be comprehensive or definitive, the following sections discuss some of the key issues regarding the costs/benefits and efficiencies/inefficiencies associated with current development patterns.

Land Rents and Other Costs for Businesses and Transportation Costs for Workers

Businesses and residents benefit from dispersed settlement patterns chiefly in terms of reduced land rents and transportation costs. Under the older technological regimes, transportation costs were much higher and proximity to efficient rail and water transportation terminals was much more valuable than it is today. Proximity to transportation terminals meant lower shipping costs, but these savings were bid away to some extent by producers competing for the limited supply of close-in sites.

After the core areas lost their locational advantage relative to port facilities, other businesses —particularly financial institutions and professional service firms—found that the regional transportation system gave core areas an edge in terms of access to the metropolitan area labor force. In other words, the established business base provided a CBD location with economic advantages. Thus, in core locations, land rents were bid up as competition for limited sites forced users to pay land rents reflecting the transportation cost savings and benefits of a central location.

Over time, however, metropolitan areas grew. Households took advantage of growing affluence and transportation improvements that made the move outward to less crowded environs more feasible; CBD space costs increased; and manufacturing establishments created a new business base in outlying areas. In response, more and more businesses found it beneficial to open either satellite facilities in these emerging suburban commercial centers or to relocate their businesses to one of several competing suburban business centers. The economic benefits to the businesses were and still are lower space costs as a result of lower land and construction costs, lower labor costs since workers could reduce travel time and save on parking and housing costs, avoidance of congestion costs associated with high-density downtowns, and often lower local taxes.

The lower cost structure for commercial, industrial, and residential uses gives U.S. firms a significant advantage over competing firms in other countries with less extensive transportation networks, less developed communication systems, fewer competing productive business locations, and general limits on urban expansion, as in Japan and Europe. Lower costs on the part of businesses mean more competitive pricing by U.S. firms, a lower cost of living for workers, and higher returns to capital and labor.

It is impossible to quantify the cost savings to businesses from the decentralization that has occurred, since it is difficult to say what the alternative would have been. If governments promulgated and enforced strict policies mandating compact development patterns, presumably office-based establishments could have been forced to locate in the traditional CBD, which, even with decentralization, would have continued to experience net growth in demand. Focusing the great share of a metropolitan area's office demand on the CBD would have forced rents up to levels that would affect the costs and amount of space demanded and, no doubt, would have triggered relocations of business to other, less costly metropolitan areas. With roughly 6.3 billion square feet of suburban office space, the rent differential of such a concentration would amount to tens of billions of dollars annually, assuming that firms could not move to another metropolitan area and avoid the higher costs. Moreover, the extended transportation system and lower-cost truck trans-

Turtle Rock at Palmer Ranch is a 558-acre residential community located within Palmer Ranch, a 10,000-acre master-planned community in central Sarasota County, Florida. The project has been billed as a community that provides a rural lifestyle in an urban context, a very attractive positioning strategy in today's market.

portation have also enabled industrial and warehouse facilities to spread out to more locations and to save money on land costs. Cost savings for these sectors are also most likely in the tens of billions of dollars.

Another area where significant benefits are associated with a dispersed metropolitan development pattern is in lower residential land rent for homebuyers and renters, enabled by improved access (lower transportation costs) to preferred housing, due to both transportation improvements and job decentralization. These primary benefits have usually been ignored in the "costs of sprawl" studies, but they are in aggregate an enormous sum.

Restrictions on the developable land supply tend to increase land prices. In metropolitan areas such as Charlotte, Houston, Atlanta, and Indianapolis, raw land costs for single-family houses typically range from $5,000 to $10,000 per unit, whereas in Seattle, Portland, San Diego, and Fort Lauderdale—areas that are generally reputed to be highly restrictive toward suburban expansion—raw land costs for single-family houses range from $15,000 to $20,000 per unit. Land price increases resulting from a constrained land supply may, however, be offset to varying degrees by the benefits associated with open-space preservation. While many studies have demonstrated that land prices increase under more restrictive land use regulations, no one has been able to measure the benefits and match them against the increased costs.

Even though development restrictions in the high-land-price areas may be justified by offsetting benefits, whether the price is worth the benefits is likely to depend on both the local situation and the circumstances of the individuals and households weighing the benefits. Existing property owners, particularly higher-income owners, are more inclined to support restrictions that yield both a windfall in the form of property value appreciation and the benefits of open-space preservation. Renters and new homebuyers, especially those in the low- to middle-income range, are more likely to question the merits of development limits.

Subsidized Demand for New Fringe Development

One of the arguments used against the current decentralized development pattern is that the broader community subsidizes new development at the fringe. Past analyses have paid special attention to such subsidies as federal tax expenditures in the form of income tax mortgage in-

terest and property tax deductions, federal highway expenditures in excess of user taxes and fees, and state and local government subsidies for infrastructure expansion to support new development.

The federal income tax deductions associated with homeownership are not technically tied to either density or location. High-rise condominiums in Manhattan or townhouses in Washington, D.C., are just as eligible for the tax benefits as a single-family detached house in Westchester County, New York, or Fairfax County, Virginia. The major purpose of the tax subsidy is to increase resident interest in maintaining and improving the house, the neighborhood, and the larger community. One could make a modest case, however, that a negative correlation exists between homeownership rates and density and between homeownership rates and age of housing. Therefore, given these conditions, the federal tax subsidy may be somewhat biased against places with higher-than-normal density and older housing and in favor of places with newer, less dense housing. The homeownership tax subsidy is not insignificant; in total, it amounted to roughly $75 billion in 1995 and, for the average new homebuyer, the benefit amounts to about $1,100 to $1,200 annually. Such a tax incentive has to be a factor in both enabling and encouraging homeownership and, given prevailing preferences, lower-density development.

However, a more important factor is that the incentive also encourages lower density at the community level because homeownership itself makes residents more protective of their investment. Homeowners are more likely to oppose higher-density housing of all types, the development of remaining open areas, and any type of massive commercial development that may negatively influence the immediate neighborhood and its residential values. One can argue legitimately that local residents are likely to discount heavily the private costs to would-be residents and property owners whose property is devalued while overstating the negative effects on local residents (voters).

Another major issue is whether automobile users are subsidized; if they are, the subsidy would have the effect of reducing automobile travel costs, thus shifting commuters away from denser housing convenient to transit and toward automobile-dependent lower-density housing. Analysts disagree on this matter. Compiling a set of coherent numbers is difficult because capital investment in new roads, road replacement, and expansion is combined with current maintenance and operating costs while user tax and fee revenues are combined with debt issuance proceeds. Thus, the asset/liability balance sheet is blended with the income/expense statement at the federal level.

Based on data from a recent report from the U.S. Department of Transportation (DOT), the annual income from highway user taxes and fees in 1993 was $70.7 billion. Of this amount, $16.4 billion was allocated to nonhighway programs, leaving $54.3 billion in highway user funds allocated to highway expenses. An additional $26.6 billion was allocated to highway programs from other revenue sources, which is reduced to $10.2 billion if the $16.4 billion is paid back. Thus, total highway revenues were $80.9 billion, with 87 percent of the funds covered by highway user fees.

On the expense side, current operating and maintenance expenses were $41.9 billion, with no charges for depreciation. DOT estimates that the annual costs in 1993 dollars to maintain the system at current performance levels will be $25 billion per year. Adding that charge as a rough estimate of current depreciation costs to the $41.9 billion yields a total annual expense of $66.9 billion, or about $3.8 billion less than the amount collected directly from highway users. Thus, based on DOT data, automobile users are paying more than the annual costs of operating and maintaining the nation's highway system.

However, the costs included in DOT's data fail to account for the sizable external costs associated with automobile use, notably air pollution and soil and water pollution caused by disposal of waste oil and junked automobiles. To the extent that these costs are assigned to taxpayers at large so that highway users are not forced to bear them, they can be viewed as subsidies of a type. It is not clear how to price these costs, but all sides seem to agree that they are legitimate costs that need to be either regulated away or taxed away via an emission or disposal tax.

Public Service Inefficiencies?

Perhaps the most common criticism of current metropolitan development patterns is that they are wasteful of public services. A dozen or so hypothetical studies of alternative development forms have provided data to show that the capital costs of less dense forms are greater on a per housing unit or per capita basis than higher-density schemes. The classic study was Real Estate Research Corporation's (RERC) 1974 study entitled "The Costs of Sprawl."

But capital costs are only part of the equation. Several cross-sectional studies of actual local government operating expenditures per capita find a positive relationship between population density and local government operating costs after controlling for other explanatory factors, including the proportion of poor population. For example, a national study of local government expenditures by Helen Ladd, published in *Urban Studies* in 1992, found that expenditures for general government services as well as for several particular services—including traffic management, waste collection and disposal, and crime control—rise with increasing density.

Another study on expenditures per capita by urban jurisdictions in Virginia found that, after controlling for population size, poverty rates, and income levels, density levels were positively correlated with expenditure levels. It appears that, as density increases, the level and range of required services change; thus, more must be spent on public services per capita. For example, higher-density development generally means a shift to higher buildings, which in turn means the addition of ladder trucks to the firefighting inventory and upgraded training of firefighters. In addition, higher density usually translates into more traffic control devices, more crime and vandalism, more problems with noise, and more police officers to maintain order and prevent crimes and vandalism.

Moreover, the "costs of sprawl" studies typically ignore long-term repair, expansion, replacement, and redevelopment costs, even though ample evidence suggests that such costs are substantially greater in higher-density environments. In older high-density communities, such cost differentials probably tend to explain in part higher expenditure levels. It is probably not happenstance that, as Figure 1 shows, high-density urbanized areas tend to have above-average costs of living while below-average density areas have below-average costs of living, as measured by the American Chamber of Commerce Researchers Association cost of living index.

A final problem that has become much less of an issue with the widespread use of exactions, impact fees, and voluntary contributions is that existing residents subsidize new residents in growing communities. With many communities financing capital facilities on a "pay as you go" basis, new residents could benefit from the use of long-lived facilities that were paid for in earlier years. Furthermore, many communities that

Figure 1
COMPARISON OF COST OF LIVING IN HIGH-DENSITY VERSUS LOW-DENSITY HIGH-GROWTH AREAS

Urbanized Area	Metropolitan Area Density 1990 (population/square mile)	Population Increase 1980–1990 (percent)	ACCRA Cost Living Index	ACCRA Housing Cost Index
High-Density Areas				
Boulder	3,071	19%	114.9	118.6
Miami–Fort Lauderdale	4,638	21%	109.8	107.3
San Diego	3,402	34%	127.5	174.1
Portland, Oregon	3,021	14%	110.3	108.4
Washington, D.C.	3,560	21%	134.2	166.8
Los Angeles	5,800	26%	125.2	158.2
Average	3,915	23%	120.3	138.9
Low-Density Areas				
Atlanta	1,898	33%	100.6	100.8
Houston	2,484	20%	98.8	91.4
Orlando	2,248	52%	99.3	93.2
Raleigh-Durham	1,739	29%	98.5	96.8
San Antonio	2,578	22%	97.4	97.1
Jacksonville	1,454	26%	96.3	86.3
Average	2,067	30%	98.5	94.3

Source: American Chamber of Commerce Researchers Association and Bureau of the Census.

assess capital contribution charges to new houses base the charges on an average cost rather than on a marginal cost. The effect of the average-cost method of financing depends on the situation. Many public service systems are somewhat "lumpy" in that the most economical design may involve building more capacity than is needed for some years. Thus, for many new users of such systems, the marginal costs of adding the user is negligible. Or, for some systems, economies of scale may result in lower average costs for all users. Accordingly, the cost burden associated with financing new infrastructure depends on the local situation with regard to impact fees and exactions, the unused capacity of the existing system, and the ability to achieve scale economies.

The Impact on Agricultural Land and Open Space

While it is easy to understand established residents' opposition to the extension of development into undeveloped forests, farmland, prairie, or desert, it is more difficult to understand the general point of view that—from an overall societal perspective—we should generally take action to stop or severely limit the conversion of open space to urban use. As mentioned above, the last census revealed that the urbanized areas within our metropolitan areas represent only 61,014 square miles out of 3,536,278 square miles of land in the United States—or about 1.7 percent of the nation's total land mass. The question, then, is how to determine the optimal amount of land to

be allocated among competing uses. Currently, about as much farmland is set aside across the nation for conservation (32 million acres) as is in urban use in metropolitan areas.

While the social benefits of increasing the amount of designated farmland and conservation areas within urban areas are several, two negative impacts are likely to arise. First, an increase will force development farther out from the center into designated development areas and corridors, resulting in metropolitan areas even more far-flung and expansive than they would be in the absence of conservation areas. Second, an increase in land setasides will drive up the cost of land by reducing the available supply of well-located land near existing nodes of economic activity, thus making housing more expensive and increasing property costs for business.

Accommodating Future Growth

Any resident of an established urban community who appreciates the beauty of the country landscape—natural or cultivated—can understand the inclination to question the wisdom of further expanding roads, subdivisions, shopping centers, and industrial and office parks into the countryside. But most people also recognize that the country is generally growing in population and must continually construct new facilities to accommodate economic growth and change. Since 1990,

13 million people have been added to the U.S. population. Our annual population growth of roughly 2.5 million people and 0.9 million households is the equivalent of adding a metropolitan area the size of San Diego or St. Louis each year. At current fertility, death, and immigration rates, the Bureau of the Census projects that the U.S. population will grow to approximately 392 million people by the year 2050, or an increase of 129 million people—50 percent over today's 263 million. That's about 50 more San Diegos or 100 Orlandos.

The above figures do not include demand for new facilities associated with net regional migration of people and businesses away from older, established urban areas and toward younger, growing areas—either at the fringe of existing areas or to smaller satellite urban centers. The residential areas in the core of the nation's metropolitan areas have tended to lose population and households while residential areas near the outer edge have tended to gain households, in part due to out-migration from the core. Net shifts in business activity are more complex. Generally, the central areas of metropolitan areas have experienced a net reduction in manufacturing and warehousing activity, as measured by a net loss of firms and jobs, but have generally gained service jobs primarily through the growth of existing firms. Thus, the recent trend has seen a net shift of activity away from central areas in sectors with a preference for lower building floor area to site area ratios. Consequently, service functions that tend to prefer higher FAR environments are likely to expand in the CBD.

With the rapid development and deployment of new communication technology and the expansion of air transportation coupled with the reduction in long-distance travel costs, recent business expansion patterns suggest that the economic advantages that drove the creation of large, center-oriented metropolitan agglomerations will no longer exist for an increasing segment of business activity. These activities will shift toward areas where the cost of doing business is lower. In a recent analysis of the effects of technology on metropolitan areas, the congressional Office of Technology Assessment (OTA) concluded:

> With technology enabling more locational freedom, the search by firms for lower-cost locations is likely to continue to reshape regional employment patterns, leading to higher rates of growth for many smaller and mid-size metros. . . .[3]

The OTA researchers then proceed to examine the impacts of technology on several major industry sectors, including financial services, telecommunications, professional services, transportation, wholesale trade, and manufacturing. They conclude that, to varying degrees and in different ways, technology is contributing to the decentralization of activity within these industries.

Thus, it seems fairly certain that the fundamental economic forces that have been determining and will continue to determine the location of new commercial and industrial space and new housing are directing that demand generally away from the older, more dense core areas of metropolitan regions and toward the fringe areas or toward smaller, newly developing urban areas where costs are low, economic opportunities are good, and quality-of-life factors are high.

Any effort to redirect this pattern in furtherance of social objectives is likely to increase direct costs to businesses and homebuyers and therefore produce negative economic consequences. Moreover, the overriding issue is that no amount of rechanneling growth is going to downplay the fact that we need to house an expanding population and a growing economy in virtually the only place where land is sufficient to accommodate most of it—at the urban fringe. We cannot reasonably house, employ, and provide services to 2.5 million new people each year simply by further "densifying" existing urbanized areas. Central cities and infill development can accommodate some of this growth, but not the vast share of it. Thus, the overarching question is not whether we continue to develop at the fringe, but how we develop. The character of new development at the fringe is the most important issue for the future. Stopping such development is not feasible as long as the U.S. population continues to grow. ✳

Notes

1. The Bureau of the Census definition of an urbanized area is an area that comprises one or more places and the adjacent densely settled surrounding territory that together have a minimum population of 50,000 persons.

2. Bureau of the Census, *1994 City and County Data Book.*

3. Office of Technology Assessment, *The Technological Reshaping of Metropolitan America,* OTA-ETI-643 (Washington, D.C.: Government Printing Office, September 1995), p. 17.